*Beyond Radical Secularism*

## Other Titles of Interest from St. Augustine's Press

Pierre Manent, *Seeing Things Politically:*
*Interviews with Bénédicte Delorme-Montini*
C.S. Lewis & Giovanni Calabria, *The Latin Letters of C.S. Lewis*
Rémi Brague, *Eccentric Culture: A Theory of Western Civilization*
Rémi Brague, *On the God of the Christians (and one or two others)*
Rémi Brague, *The Legitimacy of the Human*
Philippe Bénéton, *The Kingdom Suffereth Violence:* The Machiavelli
*/ Erasmus / More Correspondence and Other Unpublished Documents*
Roger Scruton, *An Intelligent Person's Guide to Modern Culture*
Roger Scruton, *The Meaning of Conservatism*
Albert Camus, *Christian Metaphysics and Neoplatonism*
René Girard, *A Theater of Envy: William Shakespeare*
Josef Pieper, *Tradition as Challenge*
Josef Pieper, *In Tune with the World*
Josef Pieper, *What Does "Academic" Mean?*
Leszek Kolakowski, *Religion If There Is No God . . .*
Gabriel Marcel, *Man against Mass Society*
Gerhart Niemeyer, *The Loss and Discovery of Truth*
James V. Schall, *Docilitas: On Teaching and Being Taught*
James V. Schall, *The Regensburg Lecture*
Peter Kreeft, *Socratic Logic*
Peter Kreeft, *Summa Philosophica*
Peter Kreeft, *Socrates' Childen* (in four volumes)
Max Picard, *The Flight from God*
Stanley Rosen, *Essays in Philosophy* (in two volumes)
Charles E. Rice, *Contraception and Persecution*
Roger Kimball, *The Fortunes of Permanence*
David K. O'Connor, *Plato's Bedroom*
Daniel J. Mahoney, *The Other Solzhenitsyn:*
*Telling the Truth about a Misunderstood Writer and Thinker*
John C. Calhoun, *A Disquisition on Government*
Karl Rahner, *Encounters with Silence*
Jacques Maritain, *Natural Law: Reflections on Theory and Practice*
Raissa Maritain, *We Have Been Friends Together* and
*Adventures in Grace*

Manent suggests that the intimate *union*, not *separation*, of religion and politics is the key to the European adventure. Of course, Christianity is no mere instrument of the political order: it is ultimately independent of every human order. This intimate union can readily coexist with the institutional separation of Church and state, and it makes possible the mixing of Roman virtues, such as courage and prudence, "with a faith in a God who is a friend to every person."

As Manent has stressed for 25 years now, the depoliticization of Europe has gone hand in hand with its de-Christianization. Europeans have lost faith in self-government at the same time that they "have lost faith in Providence, in the benevolence and protection of the Most High." Self-government ultimately depends upon an Aristotelian confidence in the human capacity for action and deliberation about the means to find our courage, our prudence, our justice, our moderation. But that Aristotelian confidence is powerfully sustained by faith in the primacy of the Good. Christian hope sustains action and gives us confidence in ourselves because of the benevolence of God (what the Bible calls the promises of God). Manent, then, is a partisan of both Aristotle and Christianity, since action and hope are inseparable. The nation is the crucial framework of self-government, but it should never forget its "Christian mark."

*Beyond Radical Secularism* contains beautiful reflections on the Jewish Covenant ("l'Alliance" in French). Manent pleads with contemporary Jews not to take their bearings from the ultimate crime – the *Shoah* or Holocaust – but rather to remain confident in the promises of God. It was the Jews who first brought divine friendship to nations, and we in the West must bow before this idea of the Covenant, which is not exactly rational but is not simply irrational, either. To restore the credibility of the Covenant, one must recover a sense of the dignity of the human association, the nation, "that bore the Covenant until the European arc was broken." Now that Jews have reassembled in a great, self-governing nation, Europeans can repudiate the nation only by "fatally wounding the legitimacy of Israel." That would be an affront to an admirable a vacuum. On the contrary, it has been occasioned, in part, by Manent's recognition that contemporary Europe has largely lost the capacity for collective deliberation and the action that flows from it. Europeans have tried to leave the political form of the nation behind without building "an unprecedented political form" to take its place. Rather than constructing a politically effective Europe, they have repudiated the nation and have succumbed to depoliticization. As *Beyond Radical Secularism* has it, Europeans have confused the political nation and the spiritual communion that informed it with the nation that repudiates the biblical God and embraces "the exclusive valorization of one's people." They do not appreciate the profound difference between the community of "blood and soil," which culminated in National Socialist nihilism, and the nation of a Christian mark with no "homicidal aversion for people from elsewhere." Europeans are convinced of the unique culpability of Western civilization; faced with a false choice between autochthony and rootlessness, they choose rootlessness "out of horror of a *volkisch* autochthony." The European nation, properly understood, is equidistant from both.

The principle of European history, which is ultimately stronger than the abstractions of modernity, was the effort "to govern oneself in a certain relation to the Christian proposition," Manent contends. The new political form of the nation, so distinct from the classical city and the endless extension of empire, "allowed human beings with free will and conscience to gather in political communities at once smaller in extent and more open to divine initiative." Europeans learned to govern themselves "by the guidance of one's reason and with attention to grace." The task of the nation of the Christian mark is "to find a place for the collaboration of human prudence and divine Providence." Manent observes that the theology of St. Thomas Aquinas provides the principles for this collaboration, even if it does not show "the way to put them concretely into practice."

The political form of the nation was crucial to this unprecedented collaboration between the pride of the acting citizen and the humility of the Christian. In *Beyond Radical Secularism*, characterizes theoretical modernity – its succumbing to the allure of inexorable necessity and a causality without acting men – is really an argument for moral and political abdication. Under the influence of modern theoretical currents, contemporary men and women resign themselves to a spiritually flaccid condition, neither fighting nor loving our enemies. Manent pleads against this disarmament of the human soul.

In his early writings, Manent explores the intellectual foundations and the political architecture of liberalism and the liberal state, emphasizing the self-conscious efforts of the philosophical founders of liberal modernity to separate power and opinion, and religion and politics. The "modern project," to cite Leo Strauss's suggestive formulation, began in a frontal assault on what Thomas Hobbes called "Aristotelity," the fusion of classical philosophy and Christian wisdom that hitherto had been the lifeblood of the Christian West. The liberal state, which took its bearings from a project at once philosophical and polemical, was deeply informed by the "anti-theological ire" of modern political philosophy. Taking aim at religious fanaticism and the specter of theocratic tyranny, liberal philosophers and statesmen sought to build a "neutral and agnostic state." This is a crucial moment in the modern "organization of separations," in Manent's term, a development that also includes the separation of powers and the division of labor. Of course, the modern separation of religion and politics occurred within nations that largely remained Christian. For centuries, modern agnosticism about the good life coexisted with traditional philosophical and religious affirmations. The modern world is, then, much more than an epiphenomenal expression of early modern political philosophy. The creation of a secular state need not entail a systematic effort to erase what Manent calls the "Christian mark" of Western nations – in fact, there is something "tyrannical," he insists, about that more radical understanding of secularism.

Manent has followed this intuition about the radicalization of modern secularism in his most recent work. Rather than emphasizing "separation," though, Manent stresses the necessity to think religion and politics together. This rethinking has not occurred in is replaced by evils (i.e., hunger, pain, and even death) to be avoided. Modern liberalism is, at heart, a philosophy of comfortable self-preservation that estranges men and women from the moral contents of life. True philosophy – Aristotelian philosophy, for Manent – recognizes that human things depend upon practical deliberation that "actualizes" the goods of life. And political life, political forms and regimes, depends upon an active "putting of reasons and actions in common." The common good is thus never an *a priori* Platonic Idea. For Manent, there can be no definitive or final separation of political and moral philosophy. As Aristotle famously puts it in chapter three of the third book of the *Nicomachean Ethics*, political action first and foremost involves "deliberation about means" – the means of actualizing the fixed ends of the cardinal virtues, the goodness of which is not the product of deliberation. That is, the cardinal virtues are not "values" that we valorize through arbitrary or "demonic" choice à la Weber. They are non-reducible goods – ends, which acting man attempts to actualize in the city and the soul. Manent makes this point emphatically in "Knowledge and Politics": "Whenever human beings act, the search for means proceeds by determining the appropriate proportions of courage, temperance or moderation, justice and prudence."

As an observant student of human things, Manent acknowledges "the diversity of human things, their infinite variety." Yet compared with the "strength and stability" of the basic structure of deliberation and action, these differences turn out to be paltry. Human beings, philosophers, social scientists, citizens – all can speak confidently of a common human nature, of an enduring human condition, precisely because the "pattern of practical virtues" allows us to recognize a courageous, prudent, or just person "in the human being born in the most distant and apparently different latitude."

Manent suggests that Christianity "complicated" the structure of human action by raising the great evangelical imperative to love our enemies. Is modern man still capable of hearing that commandment and acting upon it? The indifference to action that practical philosophy that shows Europe and the West that deliberation and action remain as available to us as they were to Pericles and St. Paul.

This focus on practical philosophy – on deliberation and action – has become increasingly central to Manent's work. He rejects a social science rooted in the fact-value distinction as estranged from the deliberations and choices that confront acting man. Contemporary discourses about "values" are remarkably vacuous, he maintains, since they ignore the structure of human action and render human choice arbitrary or groundless – in Max Weber's famous formulation, men choose their gods, who may turn out to be demons. Behind soft democratic relativism, with its endless evocation of arbitrary "values," lies an inexpiable "war of the gods," a neo-Nietzschean metaphysic that destroys the moral integrity of liberal democracy. Manent's thought points in a more truthful and salutary direction.

Manent's most complete and satisfying discussion of the practical philosophy of action can be found in a remarkable address on "Knowledge and Politics," which he delivered at the *École des hautes études en sciences sociales* upon his retirement from that institution in June 2014. (The text appears as an "Appendix" to *Seeing Things Politically*, published in English in 2015 by St. Augustine's Press.) Manent roots deliberation and action in the cardinal virtues of courage, moderation, justice, and prudence. It is in good action – what Aristotle calls "the rational activity of the soul" – that the human being's specific operation or task (*ergon*) is achieved. Modern philosophy, in contrast, essentially transforms human beings into "spectators," who view themselves and their actions as wholly determined by external forces or by that inexorable necessity known as History – as in the "Historical Process" or in "being on the right side of history."

This understanding of causality has done away with the human element. As Manent shows in *The City of Man*, modern political philosophers such as Thomas Hobbes and John Locke replaced action with a deterministic "flight from evil" – there is not only no *summum bonum*, or highest good, but also the full range of goods

# Introduction

CONTEMPORARY EUROPE IS WRACKED by a crisis of self-understanding. For a generation or more, the European political class has placed its hopes in the "construction" of a Europe increasingly estranged from the nations that compose it – and from the moral and spiritual contents that gave rise to the European adventure in the first place. Indeed, today's "Europe" defines itself in opposition to the old nations and the old religion that gave it life for the last millennium. Losing their political moorings and shorn of real spiritual substance, Europeans look weak in the face of Islam's self-assertion.

What Europeans need is the kind of humane, principled, scrupulous, and penetrating analysis that is all too rare today in an intellectual world tempted by the abdication of political and moral responsibility. The French political philosopher Pierre Manent is particularly well equipped to address Europe's crisis of self-confidence in a manner faithful to her best traditions. Manent, born in Toulouse, France in 1949, is perhaps the most thoughtful political philosopher writing today, in no small part because he appreciates the essential and enduring links between politics, philosophy, and religion.

In this, his latest book (originally published in France as *Situation de la France*), Manent brings together his considerable theoretical and practical concerns with rare spiritual depth. He reveals the failure of Europe's humanitarian civil religion and pleads for a restoration of prudent judgment, rooted in a searching exploration of the theological-political problem. He reveals just where the depoliticization and de-Christianization of Europe has led the continent and his native France. Refusing to despair, and not content with literary politics and facile criticism, Manent lays out a

# Table of Contents

Manufactured in the United States of America.

1  2  3  4  5  6    22  21  20  19  18  17  16

**Library of Congress Cataloging in Publication Data**
Names: Manent, Pierre, author.
Title: Beyond radical secularism : how France and the Christian
    West should    respond to the Islamic challenge / by Pierre
Manent ; translated by Ralph    Hancock; introduction by Daniel
    J. Mahoney Other titles: Situation de la France.
English
Description: 1st edition. | South Bend, Indiana: St. Augustine's
Press, 2016. | Translation of: Situation de la France; published in
    France in    2015 by Groupe Artaege, Editions Desclbee de
Brouwer. | Includes index.
Identifiers: LCCN 2016012548 | ISBN 9781587310744 (cloth-
bound: alk. paper)
Subjects: LCSH: Muslims – France – Social conditions. | Muslims
– France – Politics and government. | Islam and culture – France.
| Islam and politics – France. | Terrorism – Government policy –
France. | Religion and politics – France. | Secularism – France. |
France – Politics and government—2012– | France – Religion.
Classification: LCC DC34.5.M87 M363 2016 | DDC
305.6/97094–dc23 LC record available at
https://lccn.loc.gov/2016012548

ST. AUGUSTINE'S PRESS
www.staugustine.net

# Beyond Radical Secularism

How France and the Christian West Should
Respond to the Islamic Challenge

PIERRE MANENT

Translated by Ralph Hancock
Introduction by Daniel J. Mahoney

ST. AUGUSTINE'S PRESS
South Bend, Indiana

national effort of self-government and to whatever trust is left in the friendship of God.

Manent is a sharp critic of the radicalization of French *laïcité*, which demands much more than the separation of Church and state as formalized in the 1905 law. What it seeks is nothing less than the *neutralization* of religion in society. The old *laïcité* largely respected the Christian past of the French nation and of European civilization. French republicanism accommodated itself to a religious society, even as it affirmed a "transcendent" dimension to citizenship. The "sacred nation" and a Christian society coexisted with a lay or neutral state. These political and spiritual elements were never wholly separate, as one saw in the *l'union sacrée* that brought Catholic and secular Frenchmen together in defense of the nation during World War I. The wounds of the Dreyfus Affair were partly healed in this great *rassemblement* of the French people. The French state also never reduced itself to the single desideratum of protecting (ever-expanding) individual rights. Under Charles de Gaulle, the state embodied the dignity of France, even its "grandeur." As a statesman, de Gaulle strove to overcome divisions – partisan, religious, and ideological, Left and Right – and defended the independence of the state. The Cultural Revolution embodied by May 1968 challenged the vision of the "man of June 18th, 1940." Authority, in every aspect of state and society, came under assault, and society began to undo its bonds. The rights of man were increasingly understood in contradistinction to the rights of the citizen. Individualism went hand in hand with a theoretical and practical antinomianism. Public institutions found themselves re-defined as "docile instruments" at the service of a conception of rights that made no serious moral or civic demands.

Manent is convinced of the "vacuity" of the commonplace assumption that *laïcité* will do today with Islam "what it accomplished yesterday with Catholicism." Islam is too strong, too committed to religious truth and to religious mores, to fall prey to such individualist fantasies. Further, an epistemological error can be found at the heart of the new individualism and the new *laïcité*. Once the principle of legitimacy in Europe became an apolitical conception of human rights, in which the "individual" and "humanity" constitute the twin poles of human existence, human associations such as nations and churches cease to have an ontological or political reality. They become *"pretended realities that are only invoked to block newcomers"* – in other words, to make Muslims and others feel unwelcome. In this new ideological vulgate, the intermediate communities in which human beings really live "have no legitimacy of their own."

In contrast, Manent believes Europe can only be revivified if it takes a chance on "the old nations and the old religion." As he put it in *Seeing Things Politically*, these are "inestimable resources" for giving new life to the French and European souls. At the same time, Manent in no way repudiates the secular state, which is wholly legitimate in its own sphere. He thinks that the Catholic Church – and French Catholics – have a special role to play in recovering the link between the liberal state and the nation of a Christian mark.

The most controversial parts of *Beyond Radical Secularism* deal with French Muslims. It should be remembered that the book was written after the January 2015 terror attacks on *Charlie Hebdo* and published just two months before the even more devastating terror attacks in Paris on November 13, 2015. Upon publication, it took the country by storm. As the editors of *Commentaire* pointed out in their preface to excerpts from the book that appeared in the journal's Winter 2015–2016 edition, Manent has been accused of everything from Islamophobia to defeatism before the emerging threat of an Islamic caliphate. In truth, Manent's is a tough-minded treatment that acknowledges a *state of war* between France and radical Islam. France, in particular, and the West, in general, must prudently navigate a "high and great politics" that touches on matters of both domestic and international concern. Manent favors all the necessary political and military means to defeat the West's Islamist enemies. At the same time, he believes that France will need a *defensive politics*, since millions of Muslims already inhabit a nation of a Christian mark. It needs a *politics of the possible* that rejects every form of defeatism as well as the deceptive promises of the new *laïcité*. French Muslims will not readily become Western individualists and secularists as the partisans of the new *laïcité* falsely claim. Their way of life and moral practices are too robust, too substantial, to be dissolved by the acids of modernity. French Muslims will remain Muslims and not just individuals with rights. These are *facts* that responsible citizens and statesmen must accept and which must form the basis of a new action to form a unitary nation.

Manent thus proposes a "social contract" with French Muslims that accepts them as they are, along with their moral practices, with two notable and crucial exceptions. He argues that the burqa is inadmissible because "it prevents the exchange of signs by which a human being recognizes another human being." Europeans have never covered their faces. This "lugubrious servitude" is incompatible with a free society. France has the "right and duty to impose the most absolute prohibition on this manner of dress." The second prohibition is that of polygamy. The family, with one husband and one wife, is the building block of civil society and an indispensable pillar of a free society.

Manent recognizes that the increase in open acceptance of Muslim ways (e.g., dietary restrictions in schools, separation of boys and girls in certain social activities) comes with certain risks. Those risks can be compensated for by active efforts to preserve or reinforce the "ancient constitution" of France. To begin with, Muslims must accept that they live in a nation of a Christian mark with a strong and enduring Jewish presence. They must break with the *umma*, a universal Islamic empire, and proclaim their loyalty to France. They must wean themselves of reliance on foreign funding and repudiate extremism of every kind. Most of all, they must stop hiding behind accusations of Islamophobia. In practice, the reflexive evocation of Islamophobia has led to serious restrictions on the ability of Europeans to think, write, and speak as they please. It undermines even the minimal capacity for self-criticism in the Arab-Islamic world and among Muslims in Western countries. French Muslims accordingly see themselves as victims and involve themselves in the civic forum only to express grievances.

French Muslims must accept the fact that political rule is rigorously separated from religious commandments. Additionally, they must be welcomed into the national community *as* Muslims. By becoming active citizens, they will learn the arts of criticism and self-criticism. The compromise that Manent proposes to French Muslims grants them some of their customs and moral practices in order to invite participation in a true political body – one that is home to action and deliberation. In return, they must show that they belong to the French nation. Only a revivified nation, one that doesn't hide its Christian mark, can provide Muslims with a decent civic life.

The antinomian cultural and political enterprise that flowed from May 1968 has played itself out. Frenchmen of every stripe and religious affiliation need a "common life." The human associations – nations and churches – in which human beings actually live must receive their due. Let us cite the elegant words that conclude *Beyond Radical Secularism*: "The future of the nation of a Christian mark is a cause that brings us all together."

Pierre Manent thus provides a powerful and persuasive defense of "practical philosophy" against the regnant European civil religion and other intellectual currents that deny reasonable choice. His is a signal contribution to the human sciences. He allows us to think religion and politics together without forgetting the legitimate contribution of the secular state within its own sphere. His scholarship shows that a West that forgets classical wisdom and Christian hope, the Roman virtues and the Christian confidence in Providence that jointly animated the Western soul, is destined to succumb to lethargy or worse when confronting the challenges of the late modern world. Refusing despair, he points to the still ample moral and political resources that are capable of reinvigorating the West.

*Daniel J. Mahoney holds the Augustine Chair in Distinguished Scholarship at Assumption College in Worcester, MA. He is the author, most recently, of* The Other Solzhenitsyn: Telling the Truth about a Misunderstood Writer and Thinker *(St. Augustine's Press, 2014).*

# BEYOND RADICAL SECULARISM

# PREFACE

States are large, over-burdened beings, slow-moving, and always postponing the moment to reflect and to decide. Inertia is their rule. And yet citizens work, reflect, decide, invest, whether in their families, their associations or their enterprises. It is rare though that such individual and collective efforts manage perceptibly to modify the course or the physiognomy of the big animal. Members of society devote much of their energy to informing and educating themselves, but it seems that the being that they constitute together learns nothing at all. Only one thing seems really able to educate nations, and that is political experience, when that experience is sufficiently brutal, penetrating, and overwhelming. Eventually, as Machiavelli said, some "extrinsic accident" such as war or revolution forces the members of a nation to "recognize themselves" and to take up again the frayed reins of common life. In fear or in hope, each person is now confronted with what is held in common and what war threatens to ruin or revolution to overturn. Each in deciding for himself decides for the whole, and in deciding for the whole decides for himself. The choices made during decisive hours or weeks will long haunt the lives of individuals as well as the life of the nation, which will in truth be shaped by these decisions for several generations.

Contemporary France assumed its present form three quarters of a century ago. The experience that continues to affect our most significant attitudes and that ceaselessly animates the conversation that is the sound of a nation's soul is the defeat of June 1940. We have never got over this. Of course we have left it behind us, and, moreover, we have in a sense surmounted it, but we have never got over it. Everything that we have subsequently done, the good along with the bad, including the worst, finds its source in the defeat and the response, or the responses to the defeat.

It is by a deep necessity, and I dare say as an application of a universal truth, that contemporary France finds its center of gravity and its vector in the statesman who chose on behalf of the whole in June 1940. The "realists" who explain that we were indeed forced to accept the armistice are not mistaken in their reasoning, but they have a mutilated idea of what counts as real. The great refusal embodied by General de Gaulle "recognized" the fact of defeat much more profoundly, more lastingly, and more decisively than any accommodation with the situation as one indeed had to assess it. Only this great refusal was proportionate to the enormity of the defeat, and capable of launching and nourishing the response, which was accomplished in the founding of the Fifth Republic, but also drove a fair part of the efforts of the Fourth. The defeat was the extrinsic accident that revealed the sickness of the nation's soul, which de Gaulle always characterized as the *renunciation*. The only response adequate to the defeat had to be an ever-renewed effort to fight against renunciation. De Gaulle thus set the tonic note for the soul of the nation, by urging it tirelessly to gather itself for the political and spiritual independence of France.

To recall these things produces a strange feeling. On the one hand, we touch here at what is deepest and most sensitive in our souls; on the other, we speak of a world as distant from us as the Greeks and the Romans. The Resistance in effect embodies our last great formative experience, but, despite the commemorations, we do not know what to do with this experience, since we have renounced the effort that was a response to the defeat. We have not had another significant political experience, but this one has ceased to educate us. It is now at the mercy of public opinion, which convokes its phantoms as it wishes.

Here is an arresting contrast: the "man of June 18th" was essentially dismissed by "the events" of May 1968. In the eyes of many, these events were the decisive experience of their personal life and thus of their national life. In fact, both partisans and critics of "May '68" and what followed from it agree in emphasizing its transformative power. For the dominant social opinion, this is where the authoritative experience *for us* is to be found. We are bound up with a society that undoes its bonds, and no longer with a nation that strives for gathering and independence.

It is necessary to recognize the depth of the transformations brought about by "May '68," but it is also important to be clear about their character. Their effective truth lies in the delegitimation of collective rules, both political and merely social. The citizen of action was followed by the individual of enjoyment. These transformations are not specific to France. What is specifically French is the movement's political extremism, the dramatic confrontation between the imperious State and an unbound society, as well as the final victory of the latter despite the electoral victory of the "Gaullist" party. What is specific to France is the political victory of an essentially apolitical movement. To be sure, this movement appeared very political, even revolutionary, its various groups competing to be the most radical ideologically. In reality, as political differences were leveled in a flood of slogans, the scene was prepared for the great withdrawal of loyalty from the community, a withdrawal that would take place over the years to follow.

One might be tempted to see in these years a mere inflection of our political regime, a softening of its traits without a change in its essential features, just the Fifth Republic reaching its cruising speed. After the stress required by the General, some relaxation was deserved, and moreover very pleasant. This interpretation is plausible and reassuring, but wrong. From this moment on relaxation becomes the law of the land. It makes every constraint appear to be useless and arbitrary, in a word vexing, whether in civic or in private life. As each letting-go justifies and calls forth the next, governments are motivated to tout themselves, no longer by the guidance and the energy they give to common life, but by the "new rights" they grant to individuals and to groups. Underlying the ostentatious solicitude for the wishes of society and the desires of individuals, there is a growing incapacity to propose goals for common action. Here is the cause of the growing distance between the French and their political class. The confrontation becomes more and more tense and prickly when our representatives, incapable of presenting the nation to our view, show only themselves. And so we live, divided between our last political experience, that of the effort for independence, now almost incomprehensible, and the limitless freedom that draws us on, and that deprives any imperative for the common good of all meaning.

What has long hidden the alarming gravity of this rupture is the rise to primacy in public consciousness of what we like to call the construction of Europe. The contradiction between political legitimacy and social legitimacy has been covered over by the authority of an enterprise that delegitimized the political framework of the nation and promised an unprecedented way of bringing human beings together. While national political life was less and less satisfying, citizens and government officials looked to Europe as the natural site where freedom and government would both find a resting place. The people, unhappy with government, and the government, unhappy with the people, both turned their faces towards the promised land of Europe where each would finally be rid of the other. These sweet hopes are no longer with us. Those who govern and those who are governed remain prisoners of each other, and also, moreover, prisoners of a European Union that is now just one more insoluble problem.

If our political arrangements are condemned to this paralysis, which is sensed more and more painfully by the nation's masses, this is because of the equal strength, or weakness, of the different parties. Neither the institutions of Europe, nor the government of the nation, nor what is called civil society have enough strength or credibility to claim the attention or fix the hopes of citizens. As rich as we still are in material and intellectual resources, we are politically *without strength*. Doubtless this has not escaped the attention of those who now attack us. To be sure, when men have at each other, they do not precisely calculate the power ratios, and it happens that the weaker attacks the stronger. Still it would be a mistake to look at things in this way. When some of our citizens take up arms against us in such a brazen and implacable way, this means that, not only our State, our government, our political body, but we ourselves have lost the capacity to gather and direct our powers, to give our common life form and force.

The essay before you was written under the impression of this weakness, and it is in its own way an expression of just that. Born of the perplexity, even of the disorientation that the situation brings about in us, it is an effort to discern and to weigh the factors of this situation. In it I also hope to clarify our feelings. Not only do we not succeed in judging with confidence, but we also have trouble being clear about our feelings after so many vivid emotions. To tell the truth, our thoughts and our feelings have been eluding us for a long time. Our irritated and vacant souls are full of a jumble of historical references, positive or negative, which our experience no longer sifts or orders, and of which we make use in the most frivolous or self-interested manner. Rarely, no doubt, has the citizen, the social being had so much difficulty being sincere as today. This essay is also an exercise in sincerity. If it succeeds in bringing the reader to know better his own soul as a citizen, however he might judge my judgments, then it will have attained its main goal. In effect, without a sustained and rigorous effort of civic sincerity, we have no chance of overcoming, or even of honorably facing, the trials that are before us.

# 1.

The acts of war committed in early 2015 in Paris, Montrouge, and Vincennes can be said to have changed nothing in our country's dispositions or in its deliberations or actions. This is not the first time in recent years that cruel events, which should have profoundly transformed the moral and political landscape, have only confirmed our disconcerting immobility. The rush of emotion evoked by the event was in this case immense, to be sure, but it has proven to be just as insubstantial as its predecessors. Our representatives repeat the same empty phrases with the same ardor, and we reward them with an equally fruitless bump in popularity. Those who govern and those who are governed dutifully play their respective roles in the tragedy of a great country that refuses obstinately to take a defensive position in order not to have to admit that it has put itself in danger.

Still we have an excuse; our paralysis has an excuse. We do not know what to do because we do not know what to think. We know neither what to think nor what to do because we cannot manage to identify the problems we are presented with. Perhaps these problems will prove to be insoluble, but we will never know if we do not first identify them with precision. The first step, if we want to begin to shake off our paralysis, thus consists in discerning and setting in order the relevant elements of our situation. But it is very hard for us to describe our situation in even the most summary manner. We do not know what terms should be used to describe it, we lack the words. If, in order to analyze the same phenomenon, one person repeatedly uses the word "Islam," whereas another recommends above all that this word be avoided, it is clear that we are condemning ourselves to going around in a sterile circle, and not without the ritual exchange of offensive epithets. The civic conversation thus becomes ever more acrimonious without becoming any clearer. The ambition of these few pages is to propose an attempt to analyze our situation in such a way as to contribute at least to elaborating the terms of a useful political debate. All I ask of the reader is to finish reading this attempt before formulating his or her approval or disapproval, for what I have to say has something to please, and especially to displease, all parties.

Let's begin where we must, and where we will doubtless find ourselves once again at the end of our analysis. The first cause of the disarray that paralyses us today resides, I believe, in the very particular perplexity that we experience before the phenomenon of religion. We must start with this. To be more precise, we must observe that in general we today hardly know how to speak of religion as a social or political fact, as a collective reality, as a human association. My point here is not to deplore a lack of interest in "religious things," in the divine or in "God"; my perspective is not that of a pious person, nor that of the "believer." Nor do I mean to deplore the fact that Europeans today are generally quite ignorant of the history, the rituals and the beliefs of the various religions. My point of view is neither that of the historian nor that of the theologian. I mean to signal something quite specific and singular, something that concerns all of us as citizens and social beings.

Owing to the particular course of our history, we Europeans see religion as an individual opinion, something private, a feeling that is finally incommunicable. The power of this perspective over us is all the greater because it is essentially dictated by our political regime, and because we are good citizens. We see religion in terms set by our political regime, according to which public institutions are responsible for guaranteeing the rights of the individual, among which is the right to hold whatever opinion one wants on this world and on the other. To this decisive political cause one must add an ideological cause from which it is inseparable and which in any case consolidates its effects: what finally discourages all efforts to take religion at least a little seriously as a social and political fact is that the dominant worldview, the "enlightened" or "progressive" worldview, is quite certain that religion as a powerful or significant human motivation is a thing of the past. On this view, the proposition that any religion might have the power to motivate human beings *today*, to give them energy and direction *today*, is strictly inconceivable for an enlightened European. Humanity is irresistibly carried along by the movement of modernization, and modern humanity, humanity understood as having finally reached adulthood, is a humanity that has left religion behind.

Thus we were greatly surprised when Islam became a major factor in political life in the Muslim world, both Sunni and Shiite. Here it must be noted immediately that, until fairly recently, this world too seemed to us to be predictably following the European path; its future we saw emerging under categories more immediately intelligible for us such as Arab nationalism or Arab socialism, or in any case modernization, such concepts as drove or seemed to drive the efforts of the Shah of Iran. The victorious emergence of political Islam, which can conveniently be dated to the establishment of the Islamic Republic of Iran in 1979, was an unforeseen detour from the great narrative shared by liberals and socialists, both equally confident that religion could no longer intervene as an active political factor in world affairs. Certain specialists and bright minds quickly warned us, moreover, against the appearance of things, explaining that, behind the mask of religion, there was something else going on – beneath the appearance of something archaic, what was happening was something modern, even postmodern. Such analyses can illuminate events, and there will always be room for debate on the relations between social, political, and religious factors, as well, of course, as on the ultimate meaning of the fact of religion. But deliberation and action, unlike scholarship and science, do not have all the time in the world to reach a conclusion. Deliberation and action demand a synthetic judgment, a judgment as probable or plausible as possible, a judgment that for this reason must take account of all the various aspects of the phenomenon and thus must account as well as possible for what everybody can see; for we live and act in a common world, the world shaped by the words and deeds of human beings. And these

movements we call Islamist, which could have formulated their social and political demands in terms familiar today to people around
the world, that is, in the language of the rights of man, instead for-
mulate their demands in the language of religious law. It is by demanding that the Law of God finally govern human beings that
these movements overwhelm the Muslim world and more and more
directly and powerfully affect the life of Europe and of the West
more generally. Would it not be wise, both scientifically and politically, to revise or at least suspend the postulate, according to which
religion is destined to vanish from modern and modernizing societies?

Understandably, the perspective behind such a revision, or
merely such a suspension, is repugnant to enlightened opinion. The
enlightened view senses a palpable annoyance and must push back
vigorously against anything that questions the great progressive
narrative. We are thus assured that there is no need to revise or
even to suspend, our postulate, since religion's loss of collective
substance is still a verifiable fact where Christianity is concerned,
and since Islam's contemporary problems derive simply from certain specific difficulties that it has faced in the process of modernization. Here again the debate concerning the comparative
responses of different civilizations or religion to the demands of
modernization is quite interesting, but in the end it must be recognized that the process of modernization has now been going on for
centuries, for Islam as well as for Christianity. The argument that
explains everything by the polarity between tradition and modernity has proven to have many uses, having served to prove just
about everything and its opposite; thus it retains little analytical
acuity. As I just noted, the main features of modern politics have
long been familiar to the peoples of these regions. In any case, many
of them have performed the most characteristic gesture of modern
politics, that of claiming their collective independence, in this case
their independence in relation to a colonizing or supervisory European power. One can well argue that these movements return to
what is old or archaic only because their predecessors tried out all
the resources of modernity in vain, but this argument presupposes

that what is archaic *can* be a resource today, and that it has meaning for people who belong to our world and are familiar with its means, that they find energy and direction in it, and that religion is not the inactive vestige or the irrelevant trace to which we wish to reduce it. We ought to consider, moreover, that under the cover of progress and of science, or of such talk, we may continue to claim to exercise a particularly subtle form of domination over people we refuse to let speak for themselves, and of whom we think we know better than they what they think, what they want, and what they do. What is the relevance of a supposedly scholarly debate that is supposed to address change and yet has not changed in its terminology for decades? If the modernization that seems to us so obvious and so necessary so decidedly fails to happen over there, that is, in Islamic lands, but also in many other major areas of the world, then maybe the problem is that this modernization is neither so obvious nor so necessary as we think. In any case, I will maintain that, *in view of the practical and political question that presents itself to us*, there is nothing to gain by "looking at the question of political Islam over the long term" of the various processes – modernization, secularization, democratization – by which Europeans have striven to think through their own unique development and, by a forgivable or at least understandable extension, that of the rest of the world. Rather than attending to the past that will not pass or the future that refuses to come, it would be better to try to focus on the present, and to take up the task of seeing more clearly what it is we see.

# 2.

Let us begin then with the present configuration of affairs in our part of the world. If I were asked to point out the most salient feature in the international order as well as domestically, I would emphasize the disagreement between the average Western and the average Muslim views. The average opinion of which I speak of course involves a disposition, a way of life, a form of individual and collective self-awareness. This disagreement strikes me as a significant and tangible fact, however greatly specialists might differ on the meaning of Western modernity or of "true Islam." I believe things can be summed up briefly but impartially in the following way: whereas, "for us," society is first of all the organization and the guarantee of individual rights, "for them" it is first of all the whole set of morals and customs[1] that provides the concrete rule of a good life. Both of these perspectives on collective life are equally thinkable and livable; this is proved by the lives we live on the one hand and on the other. Each one has its strengths and weaknesses, the latter being the reverse side of the former. Let us point out the weaknesses, as befits the weak beings that we are, on both sides of this divide. European societies are based on a weak principle of cohesion; we tend radically to separate things that naturally belong together; they tend to hold together as a unity things that would be better off separate. In a word, we form society in very different ways. Why?

1   (All notes provided by Ralph Hancock and Daniel Mahoney; there are no notes in the original.) "Morals and customs" here translates the rich French term *moeurs*. There exists the corresponding English "mores," but this is now little used. We have chosen for this book to render the French word rather freely, according to context, by one of the following expressions: moral, morals and customs, moral customs, moral rule(s), moral practices, ways, way of life.

It is possible to answer this question without getting into vast historical debates, much less theological debates, but it is indispensable to note something in political history. If Europeans have governed themselves less and less by moral customs, and more and more by law and rights, this is because they have gradually built an instrument proper to themselves: the State – the modern State. This instrument is characterized by the capacity ceaselessly to modify the law of common life without ruining the collective order. In its complete form, it presents itself as the sovereign and liberal State governed according to the representative regime. If we now consider the Arab-Muslim world, we are struck by the fragility or the instability of political instrumentalities after the decline of the Ottoman empire, a fragility or instability that contrasts strikingly with the stability and the cohesive power of moral customs. Just as the perpetual changing of laws and the continual extension of individual rights leave European societies vulnerable to the vertigo of a social life deprived of all collective authority, the acknowledged failures of Arab nationalism and of Arab socialism (which have sometimes been partly mixed together) confront the Arab-Muslim world with the hypothesis or the temptation of a politics that would merge with the application of the religious law. Clearly there is no use, *for us citizens who must act in the present situation*, in placing the two types of society on some scale of progress or of "values." Whatever may be the bases of European history or the authentic interpretation of the Koran, what characterizes our common and incommunicable situation is the fact that, on the one hand as well as on the other, for "us" as well as for "them," we are facing the limit of the form of common life in which we have respectively engaged. While we for our part strive to live with no law and no moral rule other than the validation of the ever-expanding rights of the individual, they hope to find in divine law a just order that political law has too rarely or too sparingly provided. I am well aware that there are divisions on both sides. On the one hand, many Europeans are worried about the disassociation brought about by excessive claims of individual rights. On the other hand, the partisans of political Islam in the strict sense of the term are rarely in the majority in Muslim nations or societies, and many Muslims, probably most, want to live under regimes that better respect their rights; they have recently and bravely demonstrated this desire. But it remains that European worries about social dissolution and the loss of the common good are not sufficient even to slow down the promulgation of still more new rights; and in Islamic lands those who are offended by the brutality and sometimes the cruelty of Islamism already share the rule of life which the Islamists would like also to make the exclusive political law. To be sure, they reject the Islamist radicalization or exaggeration, but how could they oppose very vigorously the imposition of a law whose fundamental goodness they accept? If we are to believe the surveys conducted in 2013 by the Pew Foundation, 74% of Egyptians and 91% of Iraqi Muslims favor Sharia law becoming the law of the state. Societies tend to be moved, if not governed, by their most active and determined members, and this is as true of Europe as it is of the Arab-Muslim world. What makes communication between these two groups particularly problematic is the fact that on both sides there is a growing addiction to a unique and exclusive principle, the unlimited right of the individual in Europe and the unlimited power of Divine Law in Islamic countries. Neither of these notably incompatible principles affords much political flexibility. There was once a time when both sides shared the idea of national independence or that of the construction of socialism. These ideas may or may not be judicious or practicable, but they were held in common and communicable, up to a certain point. But what communication, what accommodation, what contact can there between the extremism of subjective rights and the extremism of an objective rule?

I have no interest in constructing a false symmetry, nor in presenting the situation in the most neutral or irenic possible fashion, and still less in highlighting an antithesis in such a way as to seal the essential incompatibility of these two worlds. Long experience provides all the proof we need of the difficulty of reconciling these two worlds, European and Arab-Muslim. Sincerely to seek reconciliation presupposes the most pertinent possible discernment of the political situation of the two worlds. Contrary to a widespread view that trusts too much in the supposedly irresistible power of globalization and democratization, today's situation is less favorable to reconciliation that was the case in other periods or in other contexts, because, as I noted above, both sides are distancing themselves ever more from a political approach to common life. In effect, whether one intends to ground social life on the exclusive principle of individual rights, or on the exclusive principle of the religious Law, in both cases one is turning one's back on the production of the common good by the community of citizens. In short, both sides are committed to a process of depoliticization. This diagnosis makes the concern that drives these pages all the more pressing, a concern that I avow torments me as a non-Muslim Frenchman, that is, the question of the best way for us Europeans to relate to those Muslims who are our fellow-citizens as well as to those who belong to an Islamic country. "To relate" to them means to achieve a little clarity concerning how to understand our relationship and a little firmness in the way we conduct it, with the hope of achieving some degree of sincere civic friendship. It also includes being attentive to the symmetrical and reciprocal effort carried out on the Muslim side.

# 3.

If the brief analysis I have proposed of our two forms of life is valid, the problem we face in practice is the following: how to accept the Muslim way of life as the way of our Muslim fellow citizens, and yet avoid this way finally being confused with the law or taking the place of the law. In this case again, and especially here, we do not have the leisure to re-write history, nor to imagine an entirely unprecedented future; we must work in the present according to what we see as we maintain our capacity to see what we see. Recent developments, in Islamic lands as well as in our own, do not suggest that the Muslim religion is about to change its status by abandoning its understanding of law as an objective rule in order to live the law as an individual right and a free choice. To be sure, some have observed that the decision to dress religiously or to enter into a process of "radicalization" results from a free act that tends to turn a believer by habit or inertia into an autonomous individual. However unfortunate may be the immediate effects of this radicalization in most cases, this personal appropriation of Islam is supposed to allow us to hope for subsequent progress towards emancipation. This argument is defensible, but it leans heavily on individual psychology and very little on collective reality. Free adherence to a community that does not encourage freedom, especially to a community that excludes freedom, reinforces this community, or this type of community, more than it favors freedom. After all, how many men freely chose to adhere to communism without rendering this movement more favorable to freedom! In any case, if there is development in this direction, it is so slow and so hesitant that it hardly matters politically for us today. We do not have the leisure to wait for history to resolve problems for us. The practical question is thus indeed the following: can European political regimes take in the Muslim way of life without finally giving this way the force of law or something like it? To be more precise: are the transformations implicit in our acceptance of Muslim ways in our country compatible with the maintenance of our political regime and of our form of society in their main features? Here I face a major objection, which I must carefully consider, since in my view it is the main intellectual and political obstacle to a judicious evaluation of the situation. It can be summed up in one term: secularism.[2]

My proposition, according to which the presence of many Muslims in Europe requires Europeans to accept as it is *the way of life shared by Muslims,* which consists in a set of constraining if not obligatory moral rules, elicits the following objection: secularism makes it possible to accept different ways of life, not as a shared way of life but as the result of the exercise of the equal right of every citizen to follow the morality of his choice, a right that our regime proudly makes it its mission to guarantee, on condition, of course, that the exercise of this right not limit the equal right of other citizens. Such, then, are the terms of the debate. Those who invoke secularism as the solution to our problems judge that Muslim ways lend themselves, when necessary, to a modification that preserves as it transforms, to a *reform* by the regime of individual rights, under which Muslim citizens henceforth exercise their subjective right, guaranteed by the secular state, to conduct themselves as they have previously been doing by obedience to an objective and quasi-obligatory moral rule. I

---

2   The French word *laïcité* refers to the separation of Church and State established by the law of December 1905. It was first imposed in a stridently aggressive manner that led to the closing of Catholic schools and religious orders. French Catholics and secularists reconciled, however, in the *union sacrée* of shared patriotism and attachment to France during the First World War. Throughout this book, Manent distinguishes between a *laïcité* that aims merely to separate Church and State and a more militant effort to neutralize religion in society as a whole. We have rendered the first, more modest meaning by "secularity," and the latter, more militant meaning by "secularism."

argue that this reform, which would constitute a kind of transubstantiation, is simply impossible, not so much because Muslim ways are not open to reform (I have no idea), but because the means of secularization is particularly ill-adapted to this end. The debate in effect concerns first of all the powers of the secular state; it turns on just what this regime or this arrangement is able to accomplish. It thus also concerns the inseparable question of the very meaning of this term, or the way in which the notion of the "secular" is to be understood. It is clear, in effect, that it is impossible to say anything about the power of secularism if one is not in possession of a clear and certain – that is, a complete – understanding of this notion.

I will thus start from the following point: the common idea of secularism, which we praise so highly for its "values" and propose to "teach," the idea from which we expect such wonders, is very abstract, and in any case very distant from the actual experience of secularity that the French in particular have known. We are right to define it by the "separation" between institutional religion and the State, or, if you will, by the religious "neutrality" of the State. This formulation, however, has nothing to say concerning the other great component of modern political organization, namely "society." But society for its part can never be "neutral." French secularity has not neutralized French society as to religion; it has remained a society of a Christian mark[3], stamped mainly but not exclusively by Catholic Christianity, including also significant Protestant and Jewish elements. What secularity has accomplished is the weakening of the social power of the Church by bringing to an end the Church's role in the State. This role may have been more decorative than real, but it appeared to be an obstacle to the

3   This is Manent's distinctive locution for indicating the character of the European nation. He eschews talk about "roots" (one can outgrow one's beginnings) and instead speaks about a nation marked or stamped by Christianity and Christian mores. He never refers to France as a "Christian nation" in no small part because of its secular State (perfectly legitimate within its own sphere) and because of the strong and welcome presence of Jews in historic France.

homogeneity of the civic body. Secularity made possible a complete educational program entirely independent of the authority of the Catholic Church. This was a considerable achievement, but it has little to do with what we have in mind and what we hope for today when we invoke the idea of secularism. What is intended today by this word is a religiously neutral *society*, one in which the greatest diversity of opinion and of religious moral practices would flourish freely, each member of society freely practicing the morality of his or her choice and "recognizing" the different practices of other members. This conception, for which many are understandably enthusiastic, has little to do, however, with the actual experience of French secularity, which has been characterized not only by the separation between Church and State, but also by collaboration and interpenetration between the secular State and a Christian society profoundly marked by Catholicism. One indication of this collaboration and interpenetration is the centrality accorded, in secular education, to the study of the "Grand Siècle," that is, the monarchical and Catholic century. We must note as well that, even though our country has known serious divisions between secular "republicans" and the "clerical" party, and even though these great parties fought intensely, sometimes even violently, over the direction the nation should take, they shared the same concern for the same nation, differently understood. Divided as parties, they shared the same France, even if they did not see it in the same light. Thus the French experience of secularity by no means provides an example of a religiously neutral common life or of a state that merely protects individual rights; instead it exhibits the following trinity: the neutral or "secular" state, a morally Christian society, and the sacred nation. These three elements, far from being "separate," were combined in a very powerful and very intimate synthesis, the highest expression of which everyone recognized to be in French literature, equally loved if not equally served by the two parties.

These remarks are sufficient to bring out the vacuity of the proposition that provides the basis of enlightened opinion, according to which secularism, as an institutional arrangement and as a set of "values," will accomplish tomorrow with Islam what it accomplished yesterday with Catholicism. An alternative would be to imagine a coming together of the secular State and a Muslim society in a renewed French nation, but this is not what the promoters of secularism have in mind. Still, we cannot rest content with this historical clarification; in any case, it must be completed. Having recalled that the French experience of secularism has very little to do with what is now meant by this term, we must now look at the problem from the other direction in order to assess how little the situation of Muslims in Europe, and especially in France, has to do with what another part, old or new, of the French population, has experienced up to this point.

# 4.

The first observation to be made is that Islam, as a human association and as a way of life, is just as external to France's history as Catholicism has been internal to it. We can certainly consider the settlement of these new populations as an opportunity for France, but if we seriously wish for this happy possibility to become a reality, then we must start by facing up to what immediately distinguishes this group, and just what makes it external to our national history. To be internal is not in itself meritorious, and to be external is no disgrace; but this difference of situation obviously has immense consequences for the social and political possibilities that are before us. In the case of Catholics at the end of the nineteenth century, there was no question of having to integrate them! It was rather a question, if not of dis-integrating them, then at least of emancipating civic life from the somewhat burdensome pressure of the Church and its "clerics," or from what was experienced as such a pressure. It is true that colonization brought about numerous contacts that led to a certain general familiarity between citizens of the old country and the populations, often Muslim, included in the French empire; these contacts included various forms of collaboration and personal friendship. However, even setting aside the conflict and violence linked with colonization, the difference of condition between the two categories of population, which defined the colonial situation, led to communities with separate lives. Many Frenchmen today, moreover, including both old inhabitants of this land as well as Muslim citizens, no doubt wish that a history so chaotic, so laden, often so cruel, could finally lead to something, to some kind of unity or friendship that would finally allow us to believe that all of that was not in vain. It is perhaps even a duty for people on both sides to hope for such an outcome. In any case, to move towards what we wish for we must start with what we observe; and what anyone can see is the long separation of populations both in colonized lands and in the Hexagon after decolonization and mass immigration, a separation that flows from the lack of participation of Muslims in French history, except as subject populations or as a long-inferior labor force. One cannot make such an observation without sadness, or even without a certain shame, but how is it possible not to see what everyone has seen and can still see? In any case, the very people who forbid us from making such observations, on the view that what is should not be, and that to honestly describe the past and the present is to "insult the future," and who at the same time noisily deplore the marginalization, stigmatization, even the "apartheid" of largely Muslim immigrant groups – does not their very indignation confirm the sad truth of our situation? One may of course weigh things on a heavenly scale and postulate that to have been on the outside or to have been left there is a sufficient reason to be accepted on the inside without hesitation, reservation or worry. For those who do not feel called to exercise final judgment over their fellow humans, this means only that addressing the problem will be especially difficult.

For at least the last thirty years, enlightened opinion has proceeded as if the solution to this problem were available, and that we sinned only by a lack of coherence or firmness in the application of this solution. In reality, we have constructed an imaginary city, this "secular Republic" through which we will bring about tomorrow a solution whose meaning we believe we have grasped and whose application to a supposedly docile part of the civic body we believe we have mastered. And yet, in the real Republic, which has been declared henceforth altogether secular, we find nothing to suggest the slightest perceptible progress on this path that we imagine we will follow tomorrow at a vigorous pace. We compare the disappointing results of our real secularity with the indeed impressive successes of an imaginary secularism. To maintain this illusion we cling to the proposition according to which for the last thirty years our country has been stuck in an increasingly noxious paralysis. This illusion yields the following formulation: "Our Republic must treat the Muslims the way the Third Republic treated the Catholics." A false idea can be deadly. I have rapidly indicated why this idea is only possible if one ignores how the Third Republic[4] actually worked and what is the real situation of French Muslims in relation to France's national life and history. Now I must look at what no doubt contributes most to sustaining the secular faith, that is, the confidence in the State that is still maintained, or at least declared, considering the State not only as a ruling and administrative power, but also as a moral and even, as it were, spiritual power. What holds up the secular argument is a declared faith in the power and the justice of the State, in its capacity at once to pacify and to bring together. Let us then consider the State in its various versions, real and imaginary, in order to determine the present situation of what has been, for four centuries, the great instrument of modern politics.

---

4   The French Third Republic lasted from 1870 until the German occupation of France in June 1940. It was marked by significant ideological polarization (between monarchists and republicans, Catholics and secularists, and the Left and the Right) and by an effort to establish a "republican education" independent of the influence of the Church. In that regard, some have called it the "republic of Kant and Comte."

# 5.

What must be observed, first of all, is that the State we expect to produce a secular society is much weaker than would be necessary for even slight success in this task. The State that is now ours, to which we would like to confide this mission, is considerably weaker than the State of the Third Republic, whose work, as we have seen, was much more limited, which is not to say easy. The big difference is that the State of the Third Republic had authority. It represented a nation that all held sacred. In consolidating public liberties and encouraging the education of the masses, it was driven by the energy of the democratic movement that at the same time it strove to guide. It presided over tangible progress in the common good. It called all male citizens to at least two years of military service. It laid down the content of education very precisely, putting the French language and French history at its center. These points do not of course say everything there is to say about the Third Republic before the Great War, which knew its own partisan divisions, corruption, social oppression, and the whole train of maladies characteristic of the political and social animal. My point has been to recall the main sources of strength, the passions, convictions, and certitudes that filled souls and hearts in that period. Our life is much more pleasant than that of Waldeck-Rousseau's contemporaries, but our State is much weaker than theirs. First of all, our State has abandoned its representative ambition and pride, thus losing a good part of its legitimacy in the eyes of citizens. The claim to represent the national community brings with it the authority to determine common goals and to focus social and political energy. By contrast, our State now obeys a principle of indeterminacy and dissipation. On the one hand, everyone looks partly towards another association of indeterminate form and status, "Europe," the main effect of which is to cause each European people to be sorry it is only what it is. On the other hand, the people as a national community being politically delegitimized and even morally disqualified, the function of politics tends to be reduced to the protection of individual rights, which themselves obey a principle of indeterminacy and limitlessness. Such a state does not consider itself authorized to require much of its citizens. Really, it demands only the payment of taxes. It has deprived itself of the great binding resource that is conscription. It has also largely deprived itself of the primordial source of civic life, that is, a truly common education designed to produce a common mind. Curiously, since the end of the 1960s, or thereabouts, almost all pedagogic innovations and educational reforms have consisted in undoing or reducing education's common or community-building features in the name of equality, an understanding of equality that henceforth extended to the aims of education: equality among levels of discourse, equality among literary genres, equality among national histories, equality between the great works and the others. . . The work of the State over the last forty years has tended to deprive education of its content, or empty these contents of what I dare call their imperatively desirable character, in order to immerse youth in distrust or indifference concerning anything that might present itself as a *discendum* – as something *to be learned*. To be sure, the zeal and the good sense of teachers, the pupils' natural desire to learn, and the residual prestige of "classical" education have prevented the *common aim* of education from dissipating entirely. It remains that the educational apparatus, with its enormous reach, tends much less to bring us together than did that of the Third Republic, which was so much smaller and which operated with comparatively very modest resources. In our day the State, when it assigns to secularism the mission of repairing the fabric of society, takes up a task that goes against everything it has declared to be desirable over the last forty years. How can we begin from the beginning, and gather children together in the competent practice of the French language, when we have done so much to strip this language of all its "privileges"? If everything tends to indicate that French has no more right to be taught and practiced than English, Breton, or Arabic, then what common purpose does education yet retain?

At a time when the State hardly knows what to teach or how to teach it, here we find it assigning teachers the mission to "teach secularism." The formula is void of meaning. If we take the word at face value, then teaching is secular when it is common to the diversity of students, taking their level into account, when it transmits the same intellectual substance because of its beautiful, true, and useful character, and when it thus brings them together by perfecting them. Now that we have done all we can in order to reduce to a minimum whatever brings us together, for fear of giving an advantage to the dominant or inherited culture, what shall we teach? Under the name of secularism we dream of a teaching without content that would effectively prepare children to be members of a formless society in which religions would be dissolved along with everything else.

Thus our State has gradually but methodically stripped itself of the resources that once made it the characteristic instrument of modern politics, one capable of carrying out the most ambitious projects, including in the event the least well considered. Though the State, as neutral among religions, obviously remains a necessary element of our regime, whatever modifications we might wish to bring about in it, it no longer has either the authority or the will to give orientation to the inner life of society. How can it propose to accomplish what the State of the Third Republic would never have envisioned, that is, the neutralization of religion in society? This idea of neutralization, which amounts to making religion *disappear* as *something social and spiritual* by transforming the objectivity of the moral rule into the subjective rights of the individual, is the imaginary transposition of a misinterpreted historical experience to a misunderstood new situation. If we want to have any chance to face up to our unprecedented situation, then we must give up pretending that the political means is already available in the form of some secularism that we have only to rediscover, renew, and teach. The situation is unprecedented, and we must develop equally unprecedented political means.

It is natural to recoil before the task, for it is one of singular breadth and difficulty. It is not only the reference to the Third Republic that we, the French, must abandon because it only misleads us. We must, more radically, register the fact that the great instrument of modern politics, that is, the sovereign liberal State, has reached its moral and, as it were, spiritual limits. The fact that the sovereign State is now up against its limits is a widely shared observation, as when we hear that globalization renders the industrial, financial, and even fiscal prerogatives of the State obsolete. How would such a weak State suddenly find the strength to give the law to religion, especially when the religion in question has no doubt concerning the legitimacy of its collective rule and when its believers have no particular reason to respect the State in question? In any case, we must not exaggerate the spiritual capacities of the modern State, even at its strongest. However impressive may have been the successes of the liberal and "democratizing" sovereign State in Europe during the three-quarters of a century between the Revolution of 1848 and the Great War, this State experienced, during this very period, an enormous political and spiritual failure upon which we must reflect. It stumbled over a religious obstacle that no one had anticipated. This left it definitively off-balance. From this stumbling finally resulted the moral and political ruin of Europe. We must pause to consider the political history of Jews in Europe.

# 6.

It has been argued – rightly, I think – that the development of anti-Semitism as an important, even a decisive, factor in European political life in second half or at the end of the nineteenth century signals the first great failure of the liberal State. It appears indeed at this time that the liberal State's guarantee of equal rights to citizens of all confessions does not succeed in preventing discrimination against Jews *in society*, whose autonomy the liberal State is supposed to respect. This discrimination is more or less disguised, and sometimes frankly declared, up to the point when explicit hostility to Jews becomes an available resource for all sorts of oppressive or tyrannical projects. This is not the place to consider the history of anti-Semitism, nor that of the Jews in the various European nations. It is certain, in any case, that the liberal or emancipatory project, famously formulated by Clermont-Tonnerre in December 1789 – "to refuse everything to Jews as a nation, and to grant everything to Jews as individuals" – proved to be a patent failure in the twentieth century, a failure that demands our attention and should enlighten us. What we find at the end of the movement towards emancipation is not Jewish "individuals" enjoying equal rights in the various European nations of which they were citizens, but rather the founding of a Jewish "nation," a *Judenstaat* that established or re-established the Jews as a political people, or that re-established the Jewish people's political condition. Many Jews are still citizens of countries of Europe, or of North or South America, but the founding of Israel profoundly changed the condition of Jews in the diaspora as well: they now had, besides the nation of their citizenship, a "refuge" and a "guardian." From the point of view of political history, what characterizes the contemporary Jewish condition is that the Jews are "contained" neither in the States (most often liberal) where the Jews of the diaspora are citizens, nor in the State of Israel, and not even in the sum of the two. In effect, by being divided between the liberal States and Israel, the Jews as a people are liberated from the very form of the State and become *as a people* a factor in world affairs. The European liberal State had failed to bring about the transformation of the Jewish way of life into the guarantee of rights to Jewish individuals as citizens. In an effort to guarantee their rights, the Jews re-established the Jewish way of life in Palestine; however, as I have said, the State of Israel does not contain all of Jewish life, which thus *takes the form of a people* that transcends all States.

The contemporary Jewish condition is in itself a subject worthy of an intensive study. I will limit myself to two remarks pertinent to my subject here. The first is suggested by the events of January. In the flood of empty and conventional talk provoked by these events, the only words that stood out, as I observed above, because they alone were marked by urgency and sincerity, were those of the President of the Republic and of the Prime Minister addressed to the Jewish citizens of our country. Sharing the same aim and addressed to the same audience, and thus intended to be exactly equivalent, the two heads of the executive branch nevertheless used different terms, and this difference is worth thinking about. While the President of the Republic addressed himself to "French citizens of Jewish confession," the Prime Minister addressed himself to the "Jews of France." The first, in accordance with the responsibility of his office, thus used the original language of the Republic, the language that Clermont-Tonnerre would have understood and approved. The second, less bound by his office, used a more direct language, a language more appropriate to the real political situation of all concerned. The difference of words reveals and allows us to assess the difference of the times. The expression that republican legitimacy would seem to require, that is, "French citizens of Jewish confession," today sounds like an obsolete abstraction, while the concrete and direct pre-Republican term, that is, "the Jews," alone seems to fit the present situation, even if it rings a little roughly in our ears. We have gone from an arrangement of legitimacy governed by the polarity between "the Republic" and "citizens of Jewish confession" – that is, the abstract order of liberalism – to an arrangement whose meaning is obscure and whose legitimacy is still undetermined, but which is governed by the more concrete and abrupt polarity between "France" and "the Jews," or "the Jews of France." Thus we have already left behind the spiritual reign of the State, or of the Republic. Under this reign, the republican State provided in principle the means of bringing together force and justice: it protected persons in giving meaning to their association. To be sure, it did not always succeed, far from it, but good citizens at least did not doubt the model. Today, not only does it fail to protect persons, as the murders of Vincennes confirmed, following those of Toulouse, but it manages less and less to give meaning to the association. "Jews" have doubts about "France," which, for its part, fears a humiliating and mutilating separation and has no idea where to look for the terms of a renewed union. The Prime Minister's spontaneous recourse to a "France" of indeterminate political content suggests that, just as the Jews have had to rediscover the continuity of their history as a people beyond the ruptures of the modern period, the French understood as an open whole must search in their history for resources that are still latent; they must bring to light forces that are still hidden, if they wish to preserve a union with their Jewish fellow-citizens, an aim for which the Republic does not suffice and of which the neutral and secular State has fallen short.

This first of the two remarks I announced is unilateral. It is the remark of a non-Jewish Frenchman, just as my earlier discussion came from a non-Muslim Frenchman. It thus demands a complement, namely, a Jewish perspective on the question before us. It is not my place to provide it, but I can try to say what a French citizen such as I am would like to be able to "expect from Jews." Since the political framework of our union is now, if not obsolete, at least inadequate, we have entered a dialogue without rules or boundaries between "the French" and "the Jews," these two spiritual quantities, or, one might say, these two "kingdoms" that are calling out to and searching for each other uncertainly. This second remark must of course be formulated with much more hesitation than the first. A certain timidity on my part is appropriate on this subject, and so I will limit myself to a single consideration. Essentially, the material and spiritual weakness of the State requires both parties to outline the contours of a new association that will no longer be simply contained in the political regime, as indispensable as that regime remains. The question that Jews must address, it seems to me, concerns the principle by which they will take part in this association, which includes along with them peoples shaped in the matrix of Christianity and thus heirs of Israel. According to the original idea of Judaism, it seems to me, if the Jews were set apart from the "nations," this was to reveal God as a friend to mankind among the nations, and to make Him present among them. The meaning of Jewish existence – if I may so express myself – is to assure the mediation between God and humanity. Of course, in the history that followed, this mediating role was appropriated and claimed by the Catholic church, reducing the Jews to the role of passive witnesses who transmitted the Books without understanding them.

The subordination of the Jews to the Christian interpretation of history is of the past, and, as I said above, the Jews once again participate directly in world affairs. The question for them is how to define the terms of this participation. The destruction of Europe's Jews put the Shoah at the center of Jewish consciousness, but also of European consciousness, or of Western consciousness in general. This legitimate and, as it were, irrepressible centrality calls for a complement. This center cannot suffice to provide the spiritual coordinates we need to orient ourselves. If, in effect, the Shoah were indeed the sole point of perspective, the association that we together constitute would be condemned to see itself and to see the world in the perspective of the ultimate crime – of the crime that was perpetrated and the crime that threatens incessantly to repeat the original crime. Humanity would be put under the shadow of the unspeakable crime that it had committed, or that it allowed to be committed, and that it risks committing or allowing once again. This configuration involves a tension that cannot be sustained indefinitely, either spiritually or therefore politically, either for the Jews or for the "nations." The new association to which "the Jews" and "France" must contribute after the manifest failure of the political matrix conceived in 1789 cannot be based on suspicious vigilance alone; it also calls for a positive principle, a principle of friendship.

Here I am obliged to make an observation that may perhaps surprise. We make very wide and even careless use of the term anti-Semitism. There is no need to enter into the history or the various meanings of this notion, but I would like to call attention to the fact that the intemperate use of this term only obscures the situation in which we find ourselves today. Pretending to be vigilant, we blindfold ourselves. Pretending to be alert to the return of the same, we are blind to the arrival of something new. Hunting down anti-Semitism springs essentially from the same anachronism as putting our faith in secularism. We have very largely left the political and moral world in which these terms had a quite clearly determinate meaning, the world in which they were deployed, along with others, in the constellation ordered by the material and spiritual power of the State. These notions are abstractions, one negative and the other positive; for under the power of the State, which itself was abstracted from society, everything tends to become an abstraction. As I have already emphasized, the new reality demands to be named more directly and concretely. It is not named directly and concretely as long as we are content to denounce anti-Semitic stereotypes.

The word that fits the new reality is the word *war*. A war against us has been declared and is happening. This is a war that sometimes targets only Jews, in which case we can speak of a war against the Jews. At other times it targets them along with Christians, blasphemers, the police, and in general the authorities and institutions of Western nations. Finally, it targets not only all of these but also the "apostate" Muslims. In such a situation, to limit oneself to denouncing anti-Semitism makes no sense at all. It is not a question of chasing away "negative stereotypes" as one does flies, and with as much success. War is not a notion; it is a certain action, or a stable and determined disposition to such action. It is very hard for us to recognize it for what it is, and thus to name it adequately, because the criteria and the sources of enmity are external to the sphere in which we have chosen to live and in which we imaginatively include the rest of humanity. The idea that we might be the object of enmity and that this enmity might be based at least in part on reasons that would have to be called religious is something we cannot conceive. We find it easier and more pleasant to believe, or to pretend to believe, that the venerable Republic is fighting an ever-recurring anti-Semitism than to consider that the whole human realm to which we belong is the object of a certain religious enmity that motivates a war in which the Jews are a permanent but not exclusive target.

The defensive war that we are up against nevertheless constitutes only half the task before us. As I have said, the other half, more intrinsically desirable but no less arduous, consists in sketching the contours of a new friendship for which the political means are not available, and which for some indeterminate period will rely more on action and on words than on institutions. Within this friendship, Jews as Jews and as a people are an essential element. The part they will now play in the world will demand of them a mediating role that might be said to correspond to the deepest vocation of Judaism.

# 7.

The density and complexity of the spiritual configuration that we are trying to unravel are such that each new path that opens up leads us towards new perplexities. Let us pause to review the main threads of our argument.

The major fact of our situation, one that has important consequences in all the domains that concern us, is the radical loss of authority by the main and decisive instrument of modern politics, that is, the State, or, if you will, in the specifically French context, the Republic. One might say, in the language of political physics, that the republican State no longer has the power either to reduce the constituent groups of France to citizen-individuals, those primordial elements of modern politics, nor to offer these individuals something to hold in common substantial enough to allow them to be true citizens, that is, *members of a larger whole*. Henceforth – to hold to the terms of this political physics – we tend to return to the pre-modern situation, that which preceded the State, a situation from which we are of course very distant in other ways. One of the distinctive features of this situation was the absence of any border between the interior and the exterior, or the vague nature of this border, or, finally, the reciprocal inclusion of the interior and the exterior. Whether the question concerns the Church, the aristocracy, or even the dynasties, these institutions were at one time at once transnational and largely independent of the state. The movement of modern politics consisted in subjecting these institutions to the State by making the State the representative instrument of the nation; thus State and nation together constituted a particularly powerful principle of unity and of life, and thus of separation from other political bodies. When this principle loses its force, the border between the interior and the exterior loses its rigor. Whether this effacing of borders is deliberate, as in the case of Europe, which wishes to bring about what is called the European Union, or simply something passively observed, as with the phenomena that we collect under the vague term "globalization," it is widely recognized as one of the most significant facts of the contemporary world.

What is often neglected, nevertheless, is that this effacing of political borders leaves religious or more generally spiritual borders largely intact; in fact, it would seem rather to reinforce them, since they tend to become the main borders. There has never been, there is not now, and there will never be a world without borders. Human beings come together in a thousand ways, and their associations are always set apart by more or less clear and distinct borders, whether these are political, religious, or based on ways of life. These various borders may overlay one another, crisscross or form the most varied geometric shapes. Today, within the territory of the European Union, the boundaries between nation-states have largely been effaced, but that has had little effect on the heterogeneity or the diversity among national ways, which persist beyond or beneath a superficial homogenization. The border between Northern and Southern Europe, though geographically vague, is nonetheless obvious to public opinion and as relevant politically as ever. These irregularities of the European terrain, which must be kept in mind, are nothing, however, in comparison with the new crystallizations that we considered above, the new spiritual crystallizations that Europe confronts, or for which it is the site. In reality, Europe finds itself the site for these crystallizations and it confronts them because they are at once interior and exterior to Europe. I will not return at this point to the tension and the uncertainty that affect the relationship between Europe and the Jewish people, even though it is in the way this relationship is conducted that the spiritual future of Europe will be decisively determined. More urgent are the decisions to be taken to guide our relationship with the Muslim world. These decisions are more urgent because they are first of all political.

For European countries, and particularly for our own, the question of Islam is a question of high and great politics because it is a question at once of the internal and the external, of domestic politics and of foreign affairs. My point is not only that this question includes aspects of domestic politics, for example concerning the authorization or prohibition of the burqa or of the headscarf in French public spaces, or of foreign policy, for example concerning diplomatic, financial, military or cultural relations with Morocco or Qatar. My point is that the two aspects are inseparable, that we cannot treat domestic questions without treating foreign questions, and vice versa. The inseparable character of the internal and the external does not make each problem more difficult to deal with; on the contrary, it would make the solution easier if we adequately understood the linkage between the two aspects or components of the presence of Islam. The truth is that the problems we face, whether they are mainly internal or mainly external, will prove insoluble if we do not succeed in developing a *coherent and stable disposition* that defines our relation to Islam as such socially, politically and spiritually. I must explain what I mean by this.

I can easily imagine the objection my readers must be burning to pose, if indeed they have followed me this far. They will say that "Islam" is not politically relevant for us, that as French citizens we know only French citizens, and that our Muslim fellow citizens, having the same rights as others, are indistinguishable from them. Thus, to include them in a discussion of "Islam" is already to discriminate and implicitly to stigmatize, and that the very inquiry I undertake, if pursued in these terms, will have the result, if it does not have the goal, of removing us from the legitimate framework of the Republic. This objection is legitimate, since it does no more than apply our political order's principle of legitimacy. Nevertheless, as I have tried to make clear from the beginning of this analysis, it is reality itself that has already become largely independent of the legitimate political order – of the Republic, or of secularism. I have emphasized that the legitimate political order does not have the capacity to do what we expect of it. This does not mean that we should renounce the Republic, and still less that we should wish to abolish it; it means rather that we must look for the means to revive the intention of the republican project in its essentials, to revive it in circumstances in which the form it has taken for two centuries has exhausted its virtues. And what is the essence of the Republican project? It is, very simply, the aim of the common good [chose commune], or of civic friendship. There is indeed a life in common or a civic friendship to work out with our Muslim fellow citizens, as with all the others; but we will have to build community and friendship on other bases than those of the secular Republic, or at least the dominant and as it were scholastic interpretation of that Republic.

Why then consider Islam as a "whole" that is both internal and external to us? Very simply because it is in effect such a "whole." It is true that this whole is heterogeneous. Even if we set aside the Islam of South-East Asia and that of the Indian subcontinent, and even if we set aside Shiite Islam, which is the religion of very few of our Muslim fellow citizens, still the Sunni Islam with which we have mainly to do consists at once of Muslim *countries*, of which the inhabitants are Arabs, Turks, Africans, etc., and Muslim *populations* established in varying numbers in European countries, and in many others besides. These Muslims practice their religion in various ways, and they may at times disagree on the right way to translate the precepts of the Koran into practice; an indeterminate number may even have abandoned their shared religion or only follow it episodically or superficially. It remains that, for most, or in any case for a number large enough to determine and fix the form of common life, Islam is still the obvious and obligatory rule of morals and customs. This rule is explicitly declared and defended as such. It is a constant theme of the daily life of Muslims, whose social and moral dispositions it informs, in particular the dispositions by which men and women conduct their relations. As I have already pointed out above, political Islam intends to make religion, not only a moral condition, and not only a constant theme of common life, but also a collective project, a great ambition, and this perspective has proven seductive for movements more or less numerous, more or less radical, and more or less violent, which act in a register that is at one and the same time religious and political, and sometimes also military. A form of morality established with the force of timeless custom and never seriously contested in its foundation, the authoritative theme of collective self-consciousness, the goal of an immense action, either current or future, that will bring back the glory of beginnings, Islam fulfills and brings together the three dimensions of human time, giving stability, compactness and completion to the *umma*. Anyone who cannot feel the community-forming power of Islam is not very attentive to the needs of humans as social beings. The heterogeneity of the Muslim world, its fragmentation, its divisions, and even internal wars do not detract from this community-forming power. And now this immense body that we thought was condemned to immobility, or even to decline, is on the move. This movement is not found either in the economic or in the scientific order, and so we are inclined to underestimate it. The point is to make Islam a protagonist to reckon with in the material and spiritual challenges that are to decide the world's fate. The point is to bring Muslims into this arena from which they have long been excluded, and where their martial virtues will finally have their revenge. The facts authorize us – no, they oblige us! – to say that Islam as such, Islam understood as a meaningful whole, is in motion, that it strives and struggles, in a word that it is an actor on the stage of history that must be taken very seriously. Thus the world in which we must live and act is a world marked by the effort, the movement, the forward thrust of Islam.

This thrust is a fact to take account of, certainly not to blame. It would be quite inappropriate for Europeans and more generally Westerners to be scandalized, since they have for four centuries been the great expansive force in the world and have for four centuries laid down the law for the world. Human things do not stand still; they go forward or backward, either momentum is on their side or it is not. As we read in Shakespeare: *there is a tide in the affairs of men*. There is an ebb and flow. There was an immense tide that came from Europe and covered the world, or almost. The shrinkage we are now witnessing is less spectacular, but it is much more significant because, rather than retracting or withdrawing the often artificial or unjust extensions of its power, Europe is disarming itself in its core. This is a demographic, political, military, and spiritual fact. Europeans now consider that their great deeds of the past brought about too many evils and crimes for it to be legitimate to want to *continue* European history. They have thus decided to draw a line and start over from zero with a historical ignorance that they are determined to preserve. This is their choice. It would make no sense for them to take offense because others, whether in Russia, in Asia, or in the Near East, make different choices, because they are ambitious, given to conquest and even violent, just as we ourselves once were, even not so long ago. They would be at fault in any case if they refused to see what is right before their eyes, that is, that others have other views and other motives, and they are arming themselves while Europeans disarm. In the case of Islam, I have just explained why it is legitimate and even necessary to consider it an important social, religious, and political fact, and now a major historical agent in the disposition of world affairs. The point is not to postulate some immutable essence of Islam, but only to recognize its existence and so to speak its consistency. As I have said, our political regime and our way of life invite us to reduce all spiritual masses to the individuals that constitute them. Finally, however, however much we may desire to see everywhere only rights-bearing subjects and individuals seeking their own interests, we run into a number of great collective facts that are decisive for world affairs. We run into them more every day. He who fears a scandal will fall on the stumbling-block of scandal.

# 8.

To describe our situation in the simplest terms of political physics would be to say something like the following: Islam is putting pressure on Europe and advancing into Europe. It is advancing into Europe by establishing numerous Muslim populations in countries such as France. It is putting pressure on Europe by the growing influence of the Gulf countries that possess unlimited capital. The situation involves a third, very specific, element that is commonly designated as Islamic terrorism. We were eager to interpret the crimes committed in January in Paris and a little afterwards in Copenhagen in a way that allowed us to keep our illusions along with our self-esteem. As in the case of President Bush and the attacks of September 11, we interpreted the massacre of the *Charlie-Hebdo* journalists as an attack on freedom or on our "values." The perpetrators justified it as punishment for blasphemers. The meaning of such acts for those who commit and inspire them is the extension into Europe of the domain of the application of Sharia law. This includes the principle of the punishment of blasphemy, which, we know, is indeed punished in a number of Muslim countries, whether officially or spontaneously, and with extremely variable degrees of severity. It is the intention of the criminal that defines the meaning of the crime, and in the case we are considering, this intention and the meaning of the crime are as clear as can be.

The three great elements that I just mentioned are obviously very different in kind. Muslim immigration, the financial influence of the Gulf countries, and Islamic terrorism are entirely distinct phenomena. They can be understood independently of each other. There has long been Muslim immigration in Europe, especially in France, without the slightest trace of Islamic terrorism, and at a time when the Gulf countries were no more than the "oil emirates."

We are right, then, to "be on guard against all conflations." But this precaution is nonetheless very insufficient. These three elements are distinct and must not be confused, but that must not prevent us from noting any links between them. For example, most of our Muslim fellow citizens have nothing to do with "Gulf money," but when this money helps to finance a mosque, or a preacher, or publishing house in France, then the two elements, in principle distinct, come together in a concrete undertaking. Likewise, when a terrorist act is committed by "an immigrant of the second or third generation," two other elements that are in principle perfectly distinct come together in this particular act. The question we are raising thus takes on a particularly poignant dimension: how could such enmity be born and grow in our midst? This does not mean that we should finally settle on the conflation that we first dismissed. It means that we must remain capable of seeing the links between factors when these links are acknowledged. If we are so troubled and so perplexed, if we search for the right words and bite our tongues, this is because these three elements are constitutive parts of our situation and of the great fact of Islam that is at the center of our struggles, for Muslims and for non-Muslims, together or separately.

The immense majority of our Muslim fellow citizens have nothing to do with terrorism, but terrorism would not be what it is, it would not have the same reach nor the same significance, if the terrorists did not belong to this population and were not our fellow citizens. These terrorist acts would simply be odious crimes subject to ordinary justice if they were not guided by an aim of war and by the intent to ruin the very possibility of a common life. In fact, the French State is in a state of war both internally and externally. It is not because of a few actions by the "unbalanced" that the French State has given military protection to the Jewish institutions of France, including especially Jewish schools. Our army has not intervened in considerable numbers and over a significant period in West Africa because of a few "lone wolves." Here we see a government normally inclined to diminish the importance of military means deploying such means on both fronts, internal and external. What can this mean, except that it is impossible to reduce the attacks upon us to individual acts without any collective meaning, and that we are involved in a war that defines a radically new situation for us? And where can this situation arise if not along the line dividing Islam and the West?

I argued above that Europeans, including especially the French, must address Islam as a phenomenon at once internal and external, and that in order to do this they must develop a *stable and coherent disposition*. Now I can be more precise: this disposition must be essentially *defensive*. This is the most important point of my argument concerning our practical and political perspective.

# 9.

The forward thrust of Islam has surprised us so much that many of us have trouble coming to terms with and soberly assessing the situation. It is clear, nevertheless, that the situation is new, that the initiative has not been ours, and that the novelty of our situation stems from the novelty of Islam's situation here in France and in the world. We therefore find ourselves in a defensive *position*. Again, we did not choose this position. This is the first time for quite a long time that something new in the West did not come from within Western life, from the internal development of Western society and politics. In any case, we must respond to this situation that we have not wished for. We must therefore *defend* ourselves. This means, more precisely: we must defend ourselves from *no other standpoint* than that of defending ourselves and preserving as much as is possible of our material, moral and spiritual goods. This self-preservation and preservation of the self's goods of course includes and calls for a self-transformation; it calls in particular for progress in self-understanding that we have the right to hope will be decisive.

Those who warn us against the idea of a "crusade" against Islam have no reason to be alarmed. The most powerful microscope or the broadest and most suspicious interpretation will not detect a single serious suggestion tending in this direction among Europe's Christians, Jews, atheists, or agnostics. We must elaborate a defensive policy; we need a defensive policy in the first place because we are weak – but strength and weakness are always relative. This decisive point must be grasped. I have tried to explain why I believe that dominant opinion was gravely mistaken when it attributed to secularism the power to transform the Muslim way of life into individual rights, based only on a little good will and the teaching of "values," and why our regime did not possess sufficient effective power to transform this way of life to the point of breaking down or sufficiently lowering the barrier that defines and separates the Muslim community. This is where we see our relative weakness internally. The point of departure of a defensive politics consists in recognizing this weakness or this impotence. Probably many of our Muslim citizens, or citizens from Muslim families, taken individually, live a way of life encouraged by the individualist society in which we live – whatever, for that matter, might be one's judgment of this way of life. Still it remains the case that, considered as a group, or as a part of French society, Muslims tend to conduct themselves as Muslims, to follow the moral practices of their religion, or in any case to honor these practices or to consider them to be what "ought to be followed." Moreover, the "radicalization" of a number of Muslims, the properly religious or "theological" character of which is rightly questioned, first appears as the abrupt re-erection of the separating barrier that they had allowed to crumble. We may grant the diversity of individual paths and the social and moral heterogeneity that exists among French Muslims, but it remains that in our country we are witnessing the extension and the consolidation of the domain of Muslim practices rather than its shrinking or relaxation. This social fact is also the major political fact that we must take into account. To take it into account is first of all to accept the fact that on this matter we have very little power. Our Muslim fellow citizens are now too numerous, Islam has too much authority, and the Republic –or France, or Europe – too little authority for things to be otherwise. I therefore conclude that our regime must *concede*, and frankly accept their ways, since the Muslims are our fellow citizens. We did not impose conditions upon their settling here, and so they have not violated them. Having been accepted as equals, they thus have every right to think that they were accepted "as they were." We cannot reverse this acceptance without breaking the tacit contract that has accompanied immigration over the last forty years. If this was a mistake, then it was one committed by all the governments in succession, and thus by all those who elected them, that is to say, by all or almost all the French. It would be very foolish to convey the idea, to seem to sanction the idea, or simply to hold the idea that the unilateral renunciation of the contract would be possible if only a somewhat energetic government, and especially a government "that listens to the French" would come to power. Maybe those guilty of this foolishness will soon be in power, or at least achieve participation in the government. They will soon learn the limits of their scope of action, and the adepts of what is "politically incorrect" will in one way or another return to the tropes of "political correctness." Even the xenophobic right is learning to be careful about what it says about Muslims.

Our Muslim fellow citizens are, then, sufficiently numerous, sufficiently confident of their rights, and sufficiently attached to their beliefs and to their way of life, that our political body has been substantially, even essentially transformed by their presence. To repeat, there is nothing we can do but accept this change. This is why I maintain that our politics can only be defensive. It will be *defensive* because we are forced to make concessions that we would rather not make, or to accept a transformation of our country that we would have preferred to avoid, and that even sometimes deeply saddens us. Still, this will be a defensive *politics* because, with all our weakness, we still have power, because we still dispose of great moral and spiritual resources that can be renewed, activated, and mobilized in order to contain this inevitable change within certain limits, and to preserve a country whose physiognomy remains recognizable. It is here that we enter into the domain of a *politics of the possible* equally distant from dreams of "fortunate diversity" and from all vague and half-repressed desires for a "return" of immigrants "to their own country."

The politics of the possible is a *compromise* between French Muslim citizens and the rest of the civic body. I will not attempt here to sketch the program of such a politics, but I maintain that this compromise will necessarily be based on two principles the value of which depends on their being honored together: on the one hand, Muslims are accepted "as they are," and we renounce the vain and somewhat condescending idea of an authoritarian "modernizing" of their way of life, to say nothing of this "reform of Islam" to which the atheists of our country aspire with a passion that is a little hard to understand. On the other hand, we preserve and defend, as an inviolable sanctuary, certain fundamental features of our regime and certain aspects of France's physiognomy. Let us now consider in order each of these two principles.

# 10.

Concerning the Muslim way of life, it is clear that the very broad acceptance that I recommend carries with it certain difficulties for the functioning of institutions and activities common to Muslim and non-Muslim French citizens, that is, for the greater part of our social institutions and activities. I do not have a sufficiently fertile imagination to conceive an arrangement that would avoid all friction in all cases. And are not frictions and difficulties the daily lot of schools and hospitals today? How might we diminish the number and attenuate the virulence of such causes of friction? It seems to me that we might be more generous in giving Muslims who wish for it the possibility to live the way of life they believe to be obligatory or desirable without hindrance or accusation. For example, it is hard for me to understand how leading politicians can include in their program of "strengthening secularism" the establishment of a single menu, with pork obligatory, for school lunches, thus confronting Muslim families with the choice between violating a dietary prohibition and withdrawing their children from the lunch program. I cannot see what good can be served by such meanness. And it seems I cannot bring myself to share the indignation some feel at the demand for different swimming pool hours for girls and boys. Is the mixing of the sexes such an absolute principle that it must admit no exception, even for the purpose of strengthening civic concord?

This last suggestion leads me to consider what seems to me the only serious objection to the approach I recommend. Such a policy risks consecrating, reinforcing and so to speak embedding in the body politic what appears to most of us to be the subordinate condition of Muslim women. This is certainly a problem that merits reflection, but it seems to me, precisely, that many who raise it are often in quite a hurry to settle it and pass judgment. Among us dominant opinion tends to be swept along by what prevails in contemporary morals. This is the only area in which ethnocentrism is not only permissible but obligatory. The question is not whether we know whether our morality is good or excellent, but rather whether it is reasonable to judge Muslim morality according to criteria that have prevailed among us for a certain amount of time, or, more precisely, whether it is reasonable to wish to reconstruct their morality according to these criteria. Again, the tacit immigration contract said nothing about Muslims having to adhere to a Western idea of relations between the sexes. What was included in this tacit contract was the exclusive legality of monogamous marriage. It is our right to prohibit polygamy and this we do, at least in principle. For the rest, the relations between the sexes are a subject of such complexity and delicacy that it is doubtless unreasonable to damn a civilization on this question.

The other prohibition that it is our right, I think, to promulgate, and which we have promulgated, if not applied, is that of the burqa. The burqa is inadmissible, not only or mainly because it affects women exclusively and thus constitutes an inequality, but first of all because it prevents the exchange of signs by which a human being recognizes another human being. It is by the face that each of us reveals himself or herself at once as a human being and as this particular human being. The visibility of the face is one of the elementary conditions of sociability, of this mutual awareness that is prior to and conditions any declaration of rights. To present visibly one's refusal to be seen is an ongoing aggression against human coexistence. Europeans have never concealed the face, except the executioner's. Indeed, human groups are rare that have imposed on themselves this lugubrious servitude. We have the right and the duty to impose the most absolute prohibition on this manner of dress. And this leads to the second principle I had announced, that of the intransigent preservation of certain characteristics of our regime and of certain features of our national physiognomy.

# 11.

The increase in open acceptance of Muslim ways that I recommend can only be envisioned if it is accompanied and compensated by the preservation or even reinforcement of certain elements of our "ancient constitution." By itself alone, such acceptance would lead to a situation in which the influence or as it were the authority of Muslim ways would penetrate the whole of our common life. The goal of the defensive politics that I am outlining is precisely to prevent such a transformation, which is in fact much less distant or unlikely than is generally thought. This transformation is now advancing under the protection of "secularism," which, always promising a transubstantiation of Islam that will never happen, has settled into a colloidal alliance with it that will last until Islam saturates the emulsion.[5] Promising a solution that is forever in the future, "secularism" prohibits any judgment on the present state of things, since the Islam we see before us is destined to be transformed into an invisible Islam; thus the restrictions now applied to Muslim practices, not very significant but vaguely vexing, are presented as the token of the great transformation that is to come. By frankly opening up space for Muslim practices, we would put ourselves in a position to judge where we stand, since we would be able to see what we see, that is, first of all, the place that Islam has assumed in the life of the nation. A correct evaluation of this place

5   By this brilliantly descriptive but, at least for the English reader, somewhat recondite metaphor, Manent refers to the delusion of secularists that Muslims are being assimilated into a "secular" society – a delusion destined to be shattered when the admixture of Islamic beliefs and ways "saturates the emulsion" and emerges as a very distinct substance.

is politically indispensable to our nation, both internally and externally.

The restrictions that I believe our political regime must impose on traditional Muslim ways thus come down, I believe, to the prohibition of polygamy and of the burqa. This is not nothing, but it is doubtless a fairly easily acceptable condition for most Muslims settled in France or likely to settle here. The second principle I have proposed concerns the preservation, or the reaffirmation, of certain constituent elements of our common life, which will perhaps be more difficult for them to accept. I see mainly two principles, and these are quite different.

The first of these is complete freedom of thought and expression. This requirement lies at the heart of modern European history. It has been discussed in all its dimensions by a number of the greatest and most diverse minds. This unlimited freedom has produced great benefits. It has also produced certain harmful effects that it is reasonable to regret. In the end the task of avoiding its dangers goes along with our freedom. What cannot be considered is to circumscribe our freedom in order to accommodate a new element of European life that lacks the habit and consequently the taste for freedom, that is, Muslims as a group sharing beliefs and a way of life. This cannot be considered, and yet this is in fact what we observe today in Europe and in North America. Under the name of "Islamophobia," what is not only criticized but repressed by a very effective censorship is freedom of thought and of speech concerning Islam; what is repressed is the capacity to treat Islam in the same way all political, philosophic, and religious elements of our society have been treated for at least two centuries. Of course this protection, or this immunity, is the worst service we could render to Islam at a time when demands for its reform are heard on all hands; the content of the reforms called for is imprecise, but they would certainly require internal as well as external criticism. This protectiveness betrays an unmistakable condescension, since it assumes that Muslims are not prepared to confront the opportunities and the risks of a free life. In any case, whether or not Muslims are ready to live in what we call an open society, it is up to us – this "us" of course includes well-disposed Muslims – to make this freedom valued and respected, and thus to put it to good use, which is not the case today. The only pre-condition for participating effectively in European society is to show one's face and to accept that our political-legal order imposes no limits on what can be thought, spoken, written, or drawn.

It is surprising to note the hesitation of important sectors of our society on this point. The motives of those who demand special protections for Muslims are varied. I will make an observation concerning the attitude of certain representatives of other religions who, in various tones, call for "respect for beliefs." The formula is very equivocal; in fact it does not hold up under examination. Beliefs are not to be respected as beliefs. If, for example, one judges the Christian belief in one God in three persons to be absurd and unworthy of a rational being, then I do not see how one could "respect" the belief in the Trinity. On the contrary, I can and must respect the person who believes in a dogma that seems absurd to me, because he is a human being and because we share the dignity of being human. This separation between a person and his opinions is by no means easy to maintain, and the masterpiece of a free society consists in knowing how to combine the vigorous criticism of opinions that seem to be false with respect for persons. We have never quite arrived at this point, and we will doubtless never get there perfectly, but this is the only reasonable and desirable perspective for the European way of life. On the other hand, the worst thing that could happen to us, and we are not very far from it, would be to live in a society in which "freedom" consists in unbridled speech that shows no respect for persons, while certain "protected areas" spread and are consolidated: in the name of respect for the practices or beliefs of certain groups, religious or otherwise, these groups will benefit from a certain privilege of immunity, or as it were extraterritoriality. We would thus be at once degraded by license and numbed by the multiplication of prohibitions.

Concerning respect for beliefs, Pope Francis made this observation following the crimes of January: "If a friend speaks ill of my mother, he can expect to get punched. You cannot provoke people by insulting their faith." I believe it is necessary to address the Holy Father's confusion between private and public life. "My" faith does not belong to me in the same way as my feelings towards my mother. Perhaps to insult what is dearest to me personally invites the kind of reaction that Pope Francis evokes, even if in practice the customs and manners of society teach us to stifle or temper the expression of anger or of indignation. Zidane's violent reaction to an insult against his mother was not unanimously approved.[6] In any case, religious issues are of another order. A religion could never be simply "my" religion. The religious association in which I participate has laws to which I owe obedience, just as the political association in which I participate has laws to which I also owe obedience. It follows that the way I respond to criticisms directed against the religion that I belong to is necessarily and legitimately regulated at once by the laws of this religion – which may enjoin me not to answer with a punch, but to turn the other cheek – and by the laws of the city of which I am a citizen, which, if it is a free city, enjoin me to respect freedom of criticism, however annoying for me the others' exercise of this freedom may sometimes be. It is precisely because the freedom to judge, and thus to criticize, has such a strong tendency to provoke passions that it is so important to obey the law that commands us to respond to critical speech, if one is to respond to it, only by critical speech. Nothing, therefore, could be more imprudent than to seem to invite members of society to conduct themselves in their public life, whether this has to do with their church, their party, or their union, with the same spontaneity and roughness that are only too natural for them in strictly private life.

This subject would merit a much fuller development, but I would like to emphasize and to repeat one point. Whoever lives in

6  During the World Cup Final against Italy in 2006, France's Zinedine Zidane, then the most famous and perhaps most respected soccer player in the world, was ejected from the game for headbutting an opponent, Marco Materazzi. Reportly the offense was a response to Materazzi's insults against Zidane's mother (or sister).

Europe must accept that the political law puts no limit on what may be thought, spoken, written, or drawn. In other ages it was possible to invest exaggerated hope in the civilizing and educative powers of an unlimited freedom, but today it would be a sign of excessive lassitude to see our freedom as only a sad necessity, even as a habit that has become dangerous. Although most members of society may practice their freedom in a very lazy way, this freedom obliges those who are a little more demanding to strive by rational arguments to persuade citizens over whom they have no power and who may at any time present the strongest and most critical and wounding objections. This is not the worst condition to live in for the thinking animals that we are, after all.

I spoke of our lassitude. This is a state of the soul that is difficult precisely to characterize, but I believe that one factor that helps explain our perplexity is in fact the lassitude of our freedom. We recognize this freedom only in its exaggerated and degraded forms of insult and obscenity. In its more regulated and more noble forms, we find freedom strangely boring; we have assumed the right to insult those whom we forbid ourselves to criticize. This is doubtless because criticism demands reasons, and because, when we think reason in general is on our side, we do not feel like having to go look for precise and serious reasons. Nothing weighs more on us, nothing saddens us more than to have to argue rationally. Mockery and sarcasm bestow the superiority of reason – only reason bestows superiority – without having to give reasons. We should not underestimate the political and social consequences of this failure. The freedom that we so easily demand is a freedom without reason, a freedom that does not need to give reasons since it always has a "right" or a "value" at its disposal; so marvelous are these claims that they are established just by being stated. This freedom that no longer gives reasons is not without affinity with the kind of religious law that essentially refuses the test of reason.

Thus the conditions of an effective and fruitful freedom are not so easy to discern or to produce. It is not enough to say in a decisive tone: here we are free, take it or leave it! The notion of freedom can become so formalistic – the formalism of "rights" or of "values" – that it leaves society weak and sluggish, incapable of governing itself with a modicum of reason. If a formally free society is not at the same time a community of experience capable of linking the three dimensions of time, it will find itself in a perpetual present where nothing really happens anymore. More precisely, it will confuse itself imaginatively with the space of the "world," in which there is nothing but dispersion on a flat surface, since any new experiences, or experiences that might be new, belong to nothing and have no memory and no projects.

In the present configuration of things, the demand for freedom of opinion and expression without restriction, as essential as it may be, as I have repeated, is not sufficient to prepare us adequately for the challenges that await us. This demand, as I have explained, is not even sufficient to produce a sufficiently enlightened freedom. The abstract principles of modern politics may be products of long experience, but they are not by themselves capable of producing the community of life and experience that they help so usefully to organize. Their abstraction, as I emphasized in discussing secularism, tends to distance us considerably from the experience that they are supposed to distill, to make us forget the meaning of this experience, and to give the illusion that we have only to apply them in order to live together freely and happily. Thus, to return to the main point of this reflection, the question for us is not simply that of inserting the Muslim community with its characteristics into the free regime with its principles, or to link the two together. I have already emphasized this, and it is no doubt a point that may surprise and offend the reader, that is, that things have already reached the point where we must accept the fact that those Muslims who wish it, doubtless the majority, will have the latitude to practice their own ways *publicly* as long as they respect the general laws of the Republic. I have argued, rightly or wrongly, that their "community," to use the current terminology, is too strong for our "secularism," and that we had best accept this fact and draw the consequences. The arrangement that I have just recalled remains, however, very insufficiently determined. It takes into account only two quite heterogeneous factors, that is, the political regime and a community of moral practices whose attachment to the regime remains problematic. The "ancient constitution" of which I spoke above, and that I believe it is important to preserve or to reinvigorate, involves much more than the democratic or republican political regime. It involves – and this is the second consecutive element that I announced – a "way of life" that is not separable from the regime but distinct from it, which conditions the regime and which, in a way, surpasses it. It is this "way of life" that we must now consider, since it is the main thing at stake in the encounter between Islam and Europe.

# 12.

Just as Islam represents for us a question of both domestic and foreign policy, as I have said, so our way of life is also determined by both internal and external factors. To state the point very succinctly, it takes both the form of a particular nation and that of European civilization. Islam presents a question to each nation, and in the event to our nation, and at the same time to our civilization, or to European history. This is no small matter.

I have assumed throughout these remarks that the relevant elements of our situation could be found to be essentially accessible to simple observation, for which the zeal and the competence of the simple "good citizen" are basically sufficient, and that we can leave to specialists the question of "true Islam," not because it is of no interest, but because it is at least not politically urgent. It is true in general, whatever the context and the problem under consideration, that it would make no sense to base a political analysis designed to illuminate action on a thesis developed from a mainly "learned" perspective, that is, a perspective inaccessible to the plain citizen, essentially contestable and subject to revision, and, especially, detached from the actual context in which political action must take its bearings. At the same time, of course, political and moral things are not readily available to everyone and "sitting there" like the pitcher on the table. Even for a person whose sole ambition is to act reasonably, political things are surrounded by an aura of uncertainty and as it were invisibility; they must be approached by a path of inquiry that, while not a matter of specialized erudition, involves discovery, questioning, hesitation, wandering, and, finally, perhaps, a wager. We experience the presence and the power of this hesitation and uncertainty, this enigmatic quality, especially when the problem concerns discerning somewhat concretely what I have called our "way of life."

When we seek an orientation in the great political question of Europe, whether the question concerns views on European unification or relations with Islam, it is clear that we have nothing pertinent to say if we refrain from advancing the slightest proposition regarding European history, but also, inversely, that we are condemned to propositions incapable of guiding political action today if we cling narrowly to a "scholarly" thesis that claims to fix Europe's "identity." We thus are in need of a certain kind of knowledge, but one I would call a frankly approximative knowledge that takes account mainly of the major facts that structure European life, major facts that are so recognized because without them the physiognomy of Europe would be unrecognizable, and because they seem to hold meaning for the past, the present, and the future. In this whole matter, where the point is to guide our action and to nourish our deliberation, propositions concerning past history motivate and encourage prudent political decision, without the latter being deducible from the former. We *hope* that the action envisioned in this way has meaning that gives meaning to the past, and that this past is meaningfully continuous with the action envisioned.

If we were to try to bring out what is essential, or at least certain essential characteristics of European political and spiritual life by contrast with certain fundamental features of Muslim life, or at least of its political framework, running the risk, to be sure, of a somewhat rough stylization, we might say something like the following. While Islam throughout its history has largely preserved the form, the impulse, and the consciousness of empire (traits which remain very noticeable, and indeed are found with renewed vigor today), Western Christianity, though born in an imperial form, and very much subject to great missionary and conquering movements, found its relative stability in a very different arrangement. The most relevant contrast politically between Christianity and Islam can be put very briefly: Islam was never able to abandon the imperial form that Christianity was never able lastingly to assume, finding its form on the contrary in the nation, or in the plurality of nations once called precisely "Christendom," then "Europe." Here a number of general remarks are necessary.

One could maintain that there are two main political forms, the city and the empire, to which it would be necessary to add the tribe, though the character of this last is only semi-political, insofar as the tribal order is confused with or mixed with the familial order. The city is all things considered the purest political form, insofar as it has no other *raison d'être* than to produce the association, or the community, whose material and moral resources are sufficient to allow citizens to lead the "good life." For this very reason it is the purest expression of human pride, in which human beings, by governing themselves, experience and freely enact their humanity. The moral character of empire is more uncertain, even suspect, insofar as the pride of domination flourishes there in an expansive movement that has no natural limits, even though, in the best case, the extent of the empire tends to coincide with a given area of civilization. To be sure, the city can be quite insolent and aggressive, as was Athens, but it retains a sense of its limits and of the limits of human things: it retains self-awareness because it governs itself. Empire can be very well and very humanely governed, as was the Roman Empire under the Antonines, but it is subject to a principle of boundlessness that prevents or hinders the mind's self-reflection. It was not only its flesh and bone, but its knowledge of the meaning of humanity, that ancient Israel preserved, in between the empires of the East, until the Western empire succeeded in destroying the Second Temple.

While empires can be more or less well governed, the expanding domination that characterizes them tends naturally to make good government difficult, in particular the government of the parts furthest from the center. This is therefore a political form that is relatively weak, or exposed to devastating weaknesses. Since empires are so extensive, one might say that they touch each other by their weak parts. Hence the enormous fluctuations of the empires of the East, as well as the amplitude of the movement of empires and the rapidity and extent of the Arab conquests in the face of the

Byzantine and Persian empires, which were weakened by their long rivalry. This is a characteristic that has ceaselessly affected the political life of Islam, what might be called the curse of extension, which brings about the fragmentation of imperial territory and often the tendency towards independence of distant provinces, which do not, however, really achieve a true independence that would remove them from the imperial form of Islam. We have seen more recently how easily Arab-Muslim countries can decide to unite, as when Syria and Egypt established the United Arab Republic, and how easily they again separate, such that the secular tendency in this civilizational area seems to be a weakness in both unity and diversity. A typical consequence of this trait, as I have said, is the abruptness of territorial changes, in particular in the form of conquests of seemingly incomprehensible extent and rapidity, as we see still today with the progress of the Islamic State.

Why did Christianity, why did Western Europe not take the form of the imperial matrix in which, after all, it was born? Why was "Rome" so different from "Byzantium"? I will touch on this question only insofar as it is strictly necessary for my argument. The fact that we as citizens cannot in any case ignore, and which is decisive for the whole development of Europe, and which, I believe, remains decisive still today for our future, is that, rather than organizing itself around a form of caesaropapism or of a Holy Empire, through a coincidence of the political association and the area of civilization, Christendom found its formula and its form in the constitution of a system of nations that we know still today under the name of "Europe." This point merits further attention.

The most widely held commonplace regarding European history is the thesis according to which the principle of the singularity of European development lies in the distinction between "God" and "Caesar," which is essential to and distinctive of Christianity. This difference of principle, it is said, prepared Europe for the institutional separation between Church and State, and in general for the freedom characteristic of the modern political order – and finally for the human rights of which we are today the fortunate beneficiaries. On the other hand, the argument continues, without even a pause to catch one's breath, the absence in Islamic lands of the principle of separation will inhibit the access of Muslims to modern liberty until the time when this handicap will be overcome by a judicious reform of the religion of Mohammed, a day we hope to be not far off. This thesis, which I have summed up a little cavalierly, but, I believe, faithfully, is too plausible not to be taken seriously. And yet at the same time it is too abstract, that is, not sufficiently political, not attentive enough to the political condition of human beings, to help us as we attempt to orient ourselves in the situation defined by an unprecedented kind of encounter between Europe and the Arab-Muslim world.

Let us first note that this thesis belongs to the family of great genealogical narratives through which Western man is pleased to admire himself, contemplating the end of history into which he has settled, and waiting only for the slower ones to kindly join him. A flattering portrait is not necessarily false, but it is suspect. In any case, considered in itself, the thesis of separation runs into two kinds of objection: those that I will call historical, and those that must be called political. For each kind, I will give only the nerve of the argument, which can be developed and modulated in a number of ways.

The objection I call historical, and which bears in any case on the history of Christianity, can be summed up as follows. Assuming that the institutional separation between politics and religion was inscribed in Christ's mysterious words concerning taxes due to Caesar, one must admit that this principle took a long time to be recognized and put into operation in the Christian world. One must admit that the "Christian centuries" long ignored what was apparently a fundamental principle of Christianity. This principle was in fact clearly set forth only after Europeans had re-founded their political order by entirely emancipating their political principles from all dependence in relation to the Christian proposition, and even from any direct connection with it. What the declarations of the rights of man say of humanity and to humanity has *nothing to do* with what Christian preaching says of and to humanity. The former tell him that he is born free and that he can and must govern himself according to this freedom, while the latter tells him that he is born a slave of sin and that he can only be freed by the grace of Christ. It is hard to believe that it was by radically separating their political principles from the principles of Christianity that Europeans brought to light, validated and put into practice the radical separation that was supposedly fundamental to that religion. This is to take Christianity to be as powerful over the world as it is ignorant of itself.

I come to the political objection that is more directly relevant to our argument: separation is not a political principle that is sufficient unto itself. If the political order and the religious order can be more or less distinct, to the point of being effectively separate in their personnel, their functions and their respective jurisdictions, they must also be in some way united if believers are to be citizens, or subjects, and citizens or subjects believers, within the same political body. As I noted with respect to French secularity, the secular State, even after the separation, was in France the instrument for governing a political body inseparable from a largely Christian nation. Whereas the notion of separation suggests the dangerously clear figure of a reciprocal exteriority, as a plane divided by a line, or a three-dimension figure divided by a plane, a more concrete perception allows us to discern a reciprocal envelopment of a largely Christian society by the Republic, or the secular State, and of the State, or secular Republic, by a largely Christian nation. This reciprocal envelopment of the political form and the regime, in this case of the Christian nation and the secular regime, presents the analytical mind with a specific challenge that necessarily calls our attention to the limits of our political axioms. Rather than seeing separation as the long-hidden or veiled secret of European development, we must instead look for what has been the principle of unity and of association of European humanity throughout our history. However useful and even necessary separation has become, it is not in itself the principle of life. Unity, or rather, the pursuit of unity, is the principle of life.

From the time the inhabitants of our continent received the Christian proposition and began to pay attention to it, they found themselves confronted with a two-fold task: they had to govern themselves, and they had to respond to the Christian proposition of a "new life," henceforth accessible to every person of good will, which consisted in participation in the very life of God in Three Persons. Both halves of this task were characterized by a high degree of indeterminacy. The task of self-government was made uncertain not only by the question of regime (monarchical, aristocratic or republican), but also by that of the political form (city, empire, or an unprecedented form to be invented). The task of responding to the Christian proposition did not come down to a choice between acceptance and refusal, since the countless heresies combatted by the Church represented so many ways of half-accepting or refusing this proposition. Given such great political as well as religious indeterminacy, so much greater was the breadth of indeterminacy that affected the articulation of the two, the difficulty of conjoining the religious and the political determination. Imagine European man of the High Middle Ages, searching restlessly among memories of Greek, Roman, and Hebrew regimes, as well as among Greek, Roman, and Hebrew political forms, required at the same time to refer to a religious proposition that was at once the most demanding and the hardest to understand ever addressed to human beings! Never was history more *open*, and Europeans have already been mistaken several times in declaring it over and done.

This was, then, the starting point and the principle of European history: *to govern oneself in a certain relation to the Christian proposition.* Now (to return to the line of argument I had begun to unfold), it was through the effort to align these two determinations that Europeans left behind the imperial matrix or renounced the project of restoring it, as they were pressed to do by prestigious memories and powerful influences. How is this defeat of the imperial idea in the West to be explained? What is the source of this interminable decay of the Holy Empire? Why was the "Roman part" so different from the "Byzantine part"? Shall we say simply that "Christianity" was incompatible with the imperial idea, or that there was an insurmountable rivalry between the empire and the

Church? And yet, the Byzantine Empire sustained a "symphony" between the two for ten centuries! Some problems are too hard. I will not venture any risky propositions.

There is one observation, though, that will help us to find our way between these two great intimidating entities. On the one hand, it is not enough to say "empire," because there are several kinds of empire. The Roman Empire emerged from the *corruption* of the Roman Republic, and yet it is from the corruption of a *Republic* that it emerged. Under the Western empire, there was always the city as a living, even if almost smothered, principle; beneath the *princeps* or *imperator*, there was the *populus romanus*. On the other hand, obedience to God's law is not all there is to Christian life. This God seeks a covenant with human beings; His grace seeks their freedom. Beneath the apparatus of the empire as well as that of the Church, there is a principle of freedom. Beneath the rivalry of two giants brimming with authority, we find the divergent and complicit operation of two principles of freedom. This operation was incompatible with the unity, the extent, and the immobility of the empire, and so progressively abandoned it in order to work itself out in the ardent pursuit of new and ever-more intimate alliances between the government of men and divine benevolence. It was necessary for human beings endowed with free will and conscience to gather in political communities at once smaller in extent and more open to divine initiative. It was necessary to govern oneself by the guidance of one's own reason and with attention to grace. It was necessary to find a place for the collaboration of human prudence and divine Providence. In this collaboration, the theology of Saint Thomas Aquinas was able to provide the principles, but not to show the way to put them concretely into practice.

Europeans thus strove to bring this collaboration to fruition in a new political form, a political form ignored by the ancients. They undertook this unprecedented political and religious project through an unprecedented political form: to govern oneself through obedience to God's benevolent intention, to seek ceaselessly to combine the pride of the citizen, or more generally of the acting human being, and the humility of the Christian. In this sense, what distinguishes Europe is not the separation between religion and politics, but rather the pursuit of an ever more intimate union between them. To be sure, this union presupposes an, as it were, infinite independence of religion in relation to every human order: the Christian Church is the only religious institution, indeed the only human association, that presents itself as *produced by a purely spiritual act, the act of faith*. This independence is at once much more than a separation, because it opens up an infinite distance; and it is the opposite of a separation because it is the condition and the cause of an unprecedented union. The movement of Christian Europe is the simultaneous pursuit of the most unfettered human action and the most intimate union with God, a union made possible and desirable by the infinite benevolence, that is, the Fatherhood of God. The object of Europe's ceaseless quest can be defined, in theological terms, as the common action of grace and of freedom and, in political terms, as the covenant between communion and freedom. The Church cannot prevent the covenant that God entered into with the old Israel, a covenant of which Israel saw itself as the sole heir, from being diffracted in Europe among several rival peoples who are equally covenanted with God. Whereas the Church saw itself as the unique path to salvation, the various nations entered into their particular covenants with the Most High, first under a Christian king, and then, after the Reformation had abolished ecclesiastical mediation, rendering the nation in a way *immediately* Christian, each as an individual immanent to itself. There is doubtless something superficial in the way we consider this rivalry among particular covenants with God as the pure and simple negation or failure of the Christian proposition of unity. After all, do we know what the effective union of grace and freedom, of communion and freedom demands? If it demands the effort of the Christian nation, then how can we condemn the rivalry of different nations? Let us not view this history from above. It is easy to see the failures and crimes in our fathers' efforts, but the profound metabolism of so many adventures that were inseparably political and spiritual escapes us. In any case, the European nation, which, beginning in the Reformation, tended to take on the attributes of the Church, remained throughout its history this kind of community of spiritual education that wove together self-government and a relation to the Christian proposition, a two-fold *intention* that opens up a plural and indefinite history, the history of European nations.

Of course, the European nations developed their respective physiognomies, their "general spirit," on the basis of various different elements, both natural, such as climate and geography, and human, with all the variety of social, moral, and political circumstances, both internal and external. If we look at European history as the result of an indefinite plurality of factors, then political and religious intentions appear as factors among a multitude of others, if they appear at all. But this way of explaining things does not make understanding possible. In effect, the bouquet of factors can be arranged in very different ways, with more or less the same plausibility. This is to retrace the time of action and of history as one would visit a building, or as one would re-build it to one's taste. This is, in particular, to proceed as if history were finished and written. Why do we so need it to be the case that the nations have had their moment and that we have left religion behind? If the notion and the thesis of separation have taken such a hold on our minds and in truth on our souls, this is because they designate the two great stakes that we have become incapable of confronting *in order to exclude them from our consideration*; thus we remain unable even to bring them adequately to mind so as to make them part of the European conversation and thus to allow Europe to remain European. Politics is "separate" from religion, to be sure, but what do we want to accomplish politically, since we are incapable of defining our community of belonging and of political action? Religion is "separated" from politics, to be sure, but what are we to make of the Christian proposition without which, either by attraction or repulsion, Europe's history loses its vigor and its meaning? Separation is a convenient shelter or alibi for Europeans who have refused for generations to pose the questions of politics and of religion without which Europe's life loses all meaning.

# 13.

Because we hold the history of Europe at a distance in this way, because we have emptied Europe of its old nations and its old religion in our imaginations, Islam's entry into European life appears to dominant opinion as *a problem that does not arise*. In an abstract social space where the sole principle of legitimacy now resides in human rights understood as the unlimited rights of individual particularity, no really significant associations or communions remain; fundamentally, none truly exists. These human associations, that is, these nations and Churches, are left with nothing but pretensions to existence. They are no longer social realities; they are, according to ruling opinion, *pretended realities* that are invoked only to block newcomers. To treat old nations or the old religion as realities that it is legitimate to take into account now amounts to *attacking* Islam. Once again, for us now, only the individual and humanity are legitimate, since intermediate communities in which human beings actually live, such as nations and Churches, have no legitimacy of their own and in fact bear the stigma of rupturing human unity. However, one might argue, this delegitimation of communities should include or implicate the Islamic community; so why is it the only one to receive the unreserved recognition and the full authority of ruling opinion?

The most decisive reason, I think, is the following. Those who decide what we have the right to say and to think do not consider Islam to be an association, or a community. It is not considered at all as a social reality. It is not considered in itself. It must be accepted without either reservation or question in order to verify the fact that Europe is indeed empty of common national or religious substance. The refusal to treat Islam as a social or more generally a human reality has nothing to do with Islam, but with Europe's self-consciousness. Thus the fact that human rights might be less well guaranteed within the Muslim association than in the old residually Christian nations does not imply any indulgence towards the latter; in fact the contrary is true. It is not a question of comparing the respective characters, including strengths and weaknesses, of the various human associations; rather it is a question of verifying the absence of anything common – political or religious – in Europe, and the unhindered presence of Islam is the supreme marker of this spiritual evisceration, precisely because it has been the supreme enemy of Christianity over the centuries, and because its moral practices are now the furthest from those of the Europe of human rights.

Here a clarification is in order. A part of the public, though very detached from the old nations as well as the old religion, looks at the Muslim association as a reality and are worried about whether human rights, and in particular the rights of women, are respected there. This opinion, which I evoked above, willingly and sincerely declares itself secular. Of course it is impossible to reduce all points of view to unity, and often judgments are quite personal. What one can no doubt say is that this secularism that is critical of Islam expresses a "cultural" attachment to European history and life, an attachment that is sincere and even lively, but that does not perhaps question itself adequately concerning the political and religious bases of European "culture," or that treats culture as a self-sufficient reality. For this very reason, as I have emphasized, it overestimates enormously the powers of secularism while underestimating Islam's capacity of resistance or affirmation. And Islam is in turn considered mainly as a "culture," in the event a culture that is hardly favorable to the rights of women.

Therefore, if we consider the two great sectors of politically correct opinion, namely, the opinion that rejects even the slightest obstacle to the establishment of Islam, and that which demands restrictions derived from the rule of secularism, Islam is not really considered as a social and political reality. Symmetrically and inseparably, Europe is considered on the one hand as empty of any common substance, and fortunately so, and on the other as a "culture" worthy of being preserved and extended. The relationship to Islam is in both cases only the shadow cast by the relationship to Europe, or of the self-consciousness of the esteemed persons of Europe. What I am trying to sketch in these pages shares the dependency I have just formulated: what I say about Islam cannot be separated from what I maintain about Europe, about its politics and its religion. If I have one ambition, it is that the analysis I propose of the European experience might be adequate to allow us to see Islam as an objective reality, instead of its remaining the reflection of our self-misunderstanding. Having emphasized the indeterminacy of European history, I will not claim to determine the truth of Islam. It too has its uncertainties and its possibilities. I wish only to help make it possible for Europeans, and especially the French, really to come to terms with Islam, and to try with its help to bring about its insertion into European life, in a way that takes account of European experience and that corresponds to Europe's vocation as it is outlined in this experience.

As I have just said, dominant opinion in Europe tends to consider Europe as a "nothing," a space empty of anything common, or at most as a "culture." I think these two interpretations are false, though to different degrees. After all, despite efforts of an almost unanimous ruling class over more than a half-century, Europeans still live mainly in their old nations, and the prospect of a leap into a post-national Europe, whatever meaning one attaches to that expression, has lost almost all plausibility. To be sure, our relationship to the nation has changed along with the nation itself. This relationship is more and more "defensive," and less and less confident and hopeful. It is more and more doleful, a suffering without hope. We have lost faith in the idea of self-government that animated European nations since they began to take form in the high Middle Ages. Simultaneously – and here I ask permission to call attention to this coincidence – we have lost faith in Providence, in the benevolence and protection of the Most High; or, if these expressions appear really too obsolete, we have lost faith in the primacy of the Good. Unlike the Americans, we no longer call upon divine protection over our nations, if we still pray for ourselves and for those close to us. How long has it been since the bishops of France prayed for France, except perhaps very rarely and timidly? I know that this question might appear strange to the reader. And yet the two operations of freedom are inseparable, as are action and hope. Every action, and especially civic or political action, is carried out in view of some good, especially in view of the common good. This common good, which depends upon us, is nevertheless bigger than us, too big for us. We are tempted to appropriate it wholly for ourselves, seeing ourselves as the exclusive authors of this good; thus the nation becomes an object of idolatry, an idol which, in the name of its incomparable particularity or its unequaled universality, demands human sacrifices. We can also, doing what depends on us as best we can, decline to appropriate this good that is greater than us, and, softening our pride a little, suspend internally our action in order to confide the common good to the Agent who is greater than any action and than any human good. As vacillating and prone to fail as we are, it makes sense to put our common goods, so mysteriously substantial and durable, under the protection and the direction of Providence: "God with us" is not only the inclination, the exaggeration and the foolishness of egoism; it can also be a natural expression of recognition for goods too great for us to be their exclusive authors. This natural movement of national appropriation of the Christian God carries a risk of paganization for Christianity, to be sure, but as citizens our part is not perfectly to imitate Divine impartiality. We address the Most High from the site of our action and for the common good of the city of which we are citizens. Moreover, Europeans never excluded their neighbors, allies, or enemies, from divine benevolence, until they were subjected to regimes that explicitly rejected the God announced in the Bible.

It can be argued that it is precisely the crimes committed by such a regime that prevents Europeans now and forever from turning to Providence with confidence and faith. It can be argued that the destruction of Europe's Jews has made it impossible to believe in this figure of the divine understood as a God who is a friend of humanity and master of history. I have already touched on this question with a trembling hand. It bears down on Europe in more ways than one. The Judge seems to be under judgment: where was He? And yet, to renounce divine Providence because of the Crime committed would only bring us back to the religion of Epicurus. This religion, the religion of the philosophers, that of the gods' indifference towards men, preceded the Shoah by a long time. If we return to it, what would we have learned from the Shoah? We would be going back to the gods of Epicurus precisely as if nothing had happened. Or would we renounce divine Providence to the point of accusing God of weakness or malevolence? Thus we would be returning, not to the philosophers' divinity, but to the impotent and ill-intentioned gods of paganism. Both the God of the philosophers and the learned and the God of Abraham, Isaac, and Jacob would lose their meaning.

If we do not give up on life, we must act. In order to act, we must have confidence in the possibility of the good. Why forbid ourselves out of conscience to follow this confidence all the way? It seems to me, in any case, that if we do not succeed in turning once more with confidence towards the possibility of the Good, or at least in tracing this movement of the heart, we will not recover the desire to govern ourselves and the confidence in our own powers that alone can nourish this desire. The idea of acting for the common good has lost its meaning for us. We do whatever it is we do, not because it is useful, honest or noble, but because it is necessary, because *we cannot do otherwise*. In the name of a global marketplace, we have constructed a system of action that can best be described as an artificial Providence: at once the only thing we can do and the best that we can do is to respond with docility to the indications of the global marketplace, each indication having the superhuman force and authority of the Whole on its side. My how we love this providence! How docile we are when its hand comes down on us! And how the wise and powerful know to interpret its dictates! Never have there been so few arguments against divine Providence, since we have organized ourselves in order to have less and less need of free will, in order to have less and less need to carry out a complete action, that is, one oriented by the idea of a good desirable in itself, since we no longer want to act except as driven by necessity. We will not be able to re-open the domain of action if we do not dissipate the prestige of this false providence, if we do not recover a reflection on the political order as the framework and the product of choice for the common good, if we do not rediscover the desire and hope of the Covenant.

# 14.

Islam will not enter into Europe simply by advancing in the field of human rights, a field void of common substance, passively open to all new contents. Nor will it come to enrich or to trouble European culture, which is too indeterminate a category politically to provide a basis for action. It will be or will not be received, it will be well or badly received in the various European nations, according to whether these nations recover or do not recover their capacities for action. Contrary to what almost all the parties think, the sole chance for Islam's tolerably successful participation in European life lies in the revival of nations and not in their effacement. Islam can only be received within a community of action that engages it and essentially obliges it to participate in what is common; in an arrangement without a common goal, one that merely guarantees and respects human rights, it can never be more than suffered.

Successive governments have given up addressing the Muslims of France as participants in a common action because they have renounced the very idea of a common action of which "France" would be the element, the agent, and the object. Since for them there is no question of *acting with* Muslims, and since Muslims nevertheless make up part of national life, it remains only to make them disappear by making everything disappear that, despite everything, still constitutes what is held in common for us as a country. This act of prestidigitation is obviously of extreme difficulty, and it must ever be repeated. In any case, the governments that long ago renounced the ambition to guide our actions are full of zeal to organize our perceptions. In truth, they intend to decide what it is we see. Since perceptions have no social existence except through speech, the problem is to control speech severely. How can Muslims in France be made to disappear by the magic of a turn of language? The first step consists in not naming those who are not Muslim, for to name them would give substance to a numerous group from which Muslims would thus be excluded. To this end, the naming of all common things in which Muslims do not take part must be avoided, since they can be said to be excluded from them, even though it is up to no one but them to be included. This is particularly true of Christianity, which we have seen the President of the Republic avoid naming even when it would be natural and even necessary to name it. In any case, the old inhabitants of this country cannot be named by any of their collective affiliations, and by so designating them, I confess that I am breaking the rule. But if those who are not Muslims cannot be named, then the only participants in social life that can be named are Muslims themselves, and so, even though it was hoped they would disappear from the scene, they are the only ones with a legitimate name. What is to be done? How can Muslims be made to disappear just like non-Muslims? Well, by prohibiting that they be named, too! But how can we avoid naming them when we are otherwise so concerned to guarantee and verify that their rights as citizens are respected?

We have thus borrowed from Islamic propaganda the notion of Islamophobia that now plays a major and troubling role in our social and political life. It has no meaning, but it has a function. The notion of Islamophobia makes it possible tendentiously to disqualify all speech on Islam or on the Muslims. Anyone who begins a sentence by the term "Muslims" knows that he must be careful about the words that follow, for an offense is in the making. It is possible to speak calmly of Muslims only in order to give voice to legitimate complaints that they address or could address to the rest of the social body, which then might be named. We can speak of Muslims to say that they have too few mosques and of Christians to say that they have too many churches. We thus postulate that Muslims open their mouths in society only to state legitimate complaints, and that the legitimate speech of Muslims is only an accompaniment of their legitimate complaints. Once the notion of Islamophobia is established and validated, it is impossible to speak of Muslims except to state their grievances, and they cannot speak except to complain. It is not surprising that they give in to this temptation, but it is surprising that the governments that give currency and validity to this notion do not realize the harm they are doing to the social body, and to Muslims first of all. Even as we claim to reduce all the criteria of common life to equality alone, we are confining Muslims to a general and perpetual status as minors. They are excluded from equality on the premise that they are incapable of taking part normally in social life, and especially in discourse and in the exchange of opinions. It goes without saying that, insofar as there indeed exist hostile, or at least distrustful and apprehensive, dispositions or feelings in the social body as concerns Muslims, the attempt to hunt down imaginary Islamophobia can only cover up, reinforce, and further poison these quite real dispositions or feelings. By their determination to lay down the law concerning social perceptions and the words that translate them, our governments are increasingly abandoning the domain of actual political action. They proceed as if social life were a *spectacle* and as if the parts of the body politic were objects the perception of which were subject to command: politics becomes a *mise en scène*. Through ever more emphatic words and gestures, they go to great lengths to command us not to see.

This ridiculous tyranny affects our Muslim citizens as well, forcing them, too, to live on this artificial stage, the vanity of which is as evident to them as to anyone. It is true, as I said, that their first movement is often to take advantage of this arrangement, and to enter into the role that is offered to them. In so doing, moreover, they are only participating in the great game of complaint that has for some time been the preferred vocal register of the constituent groups of our society. Who among us is not, as a member of a group, the unfortunate victim of a crime, or at least an offense against equality, or an historical offense, or a lack of respect? I am not sure that the Muslims of France are the most frequent or strident complainers. In any case, the transformation of the public conversation into a tearful quarrel has deleterious consequences for society as a whole and for each of its parts, consequences that are all the more serious for those parts that are more distant from the heart of national life. Here we touch on one of the great weak points of the contemporary social and moral arrangement. This merits further attention.

# 15.

In order to appreciate what is distinctive in the present arrangement, it is useful to compare it briefly to the arrangement of claims that preceded it. All claims, everywhere and always, invoke a lack, an injustice, or an offense suffered, a right denied. This was as true of the social claims of yesterday as it is of today's religious or "cultural" claims. There is, nevertheless, a great difference between the two types of claims. The social movements summed up in the word "socialism" were driven by an affirmation concerning the social truth. They affirmed that common life had to be remade on the basis of class condition, which raised a two-fold question: it was asked what part the proletarians as proletarians were supposed to play in common life, and inseparably it was also asked in what way common life was supposed to be proletarian. Socialism considered the life and the action of the group of the "exploited" within a perspective of the positive transformation of the social whole. Contemporary claims are of a very different kind, and it is striking, moreover, that claims of the socialist kind have become unintelligible for us, including for the parties that still call themselves socialist. Today's claims aim directly at no transformation of the social whole, which they do not at all have in view or take into consideration. They are, as it were, circular or self-referential. There is still the demand that an injustice suffered be rectified, but in view of what, for the purpose of what transformation of common life – these questions are left completely undetermined. It is postulated that the rectification of injustice suffices to itself, as if the considered group were not part of a social whole with which it interacted. We proceed as if there were no social and political life, but a state of affairs that a detached observer might look over in order simply to verify that equality is properly respected. But what equality is this, when we ignore the form of the society in which one is supposed to arrive at equality? In the case that interests us most particularly, what does equality mean for the Muslim citizens of France? If we understand this problem as a simple problem of equality of rights, we remain prisoners of an essentially inadequate approach, since the decisive question is the form of common life.

If now, in order to shed light on our perplexity, we take advantage of the comparison I introduced above, we might say something like the following: Just as socialism asked itself what part the proletarians should play in the common life and what proletarian character this common life should take on, we would all benefit if our Muslim fellow citizens asked themselves what part they wished to take in the common life of our country, and inseparably – but this question is for all citizens – what transformation of the common life we should expect, that is, hope for or fear, from this participation. To be sure, membership in a class and religious membership are very different factors, but they imply sufficiently analogous problems for the two sorts of groups that it is useful to compare them. In both cases, claims are deployed over an extremely wide range. The range of claims is richly documented in the case of social movements that confronted the effects of capitalism. This range went from the most timid reformism to the most ambitious project of revolutionary transformation. Now, what makes the assessment of collective perspectives particularly tricky in the case of Muslims in France is that we have only a very vague and incomplete knowledge of the extent of their claims. The arrangement of which I spoke above incites us as well as them to reduce their claims to the demand for equality, and we have emphasized the narrowness and indeterminacy of this claim, which, in addition, confines Muslims to an almost entirely passive role. Leaving aside the two extremes, on the one hand those who, whatever their relation to Islam, have simply entered into French society and have become "indistinguishable," and on the other those who on the contrary see themselves as at war against the infidels and declare themselves "enemies," most Muslims seem to remain in a condition that is too passive and too inarticulate to know with any clarity what they want and how they would respond to the double question that we are posing. The strictly self-referential claims, such as the demand that mosques be built, shed no light on their effective dispositions towards the whole that we together constitute. This passive and taciturn quality of French Islam makes up a main part of the problem of Islam in France and for France.

This characterization is not intended as a reproach. It is expected that newcomers in a country remain particularly discreet for some time, and given recent and cruel conflicts, especially the Algerian war, this reserve is still more understandable. But finally the newcomers are no longer so new, and if they remain aloof, then that has as much to do with the way society as a whole understands itself as with their particular situation. Often with the best intentions in the world, we dissuade them from expressing themselves with candor. As we wish to be only individuals without significant attachments, we want to see around us only such individuals, and even though this social commandment cannot deeply transform the substance of the group, it is sufficiently intimidating to shape the way that this substance is expressed. As I said very early in this essay, our regime's formula for legitimacy, at least as we understand it today, prevents us from looking at Islam in France as a social fact determined by moral practices. Our misunderstanding of their collective existence hardly helps them to express this existence with a view to the social whole, and we, on both sides, bridge the resulting gap through an intemperate resort to the language of rights, which only aggravates the misunderstanding. Those who speak only the language of individual rights will never treat a social or political problem pertinently.

Our Muslim fellow citizens will be able to raise the question of their relationship to the social and political whole only if the question of the whole is raised by all, and this over the whole range of the political body. If we remain enslaved to the exclusive perspective of individual rights, whatever the fortune or misfortune of the Muslims of France concerning their access to equality with their fellow citizens, we will not even touch the problem of Muslims as it concerns their participation in the common life. This problem will no doubt continue to get worse by the spread and the consolidation of what is called a "morality-based group" that very simply will have no place in the whole, and so will have no way to speak for itself within the whole that itself remains inarticulate because it does not understand itself as a whole. Such a group will be more and more confined within a traditional or immanent self-understanding, precisely as a group defined merely by its moral practices, even as an indeterminate number of its members will strive by violent gestures or acts of war to overcome the yawning gap established between its moral practices and the faceless society of rights-bearing individuals. If we do nothing, in a society that sees itself as dust, the Muslims will tend more and more to be a distinctly solid and compact element, while neither they nor their fellow citizens will be capable of giving meaning to a coexistence between heterogeneous ways of life, a coexistence that will be as difficult to conceptualize as it is inconvenient to live. And surely there is no need to emphasize the dangers inherent in such a situation. What then is to be done?

Muslims will be able to leave behind the immanence of traditional moral practices only if society as a whole, if the political body in its entirety, rids itself of the immanence of rights and of their now exclusive authority, only if we succeed in reviving representation, the consciousness and the will of a common life, the feeling that it is desirable to participate in a form of life. Our rights do not provide us with a form. At most – and this is not insignificant – they facilitate or enlarge our participation in an old form, if there is already one present, or a new one if the new rights are a factor in producing it. Many have hoped that the rights of man, once turned against the national attachment the founding of which they made possible in 1789, would give access to a new political form, the European form. The present state of the European Union, marked by heterogeneity, inequality and domination by a "center" without definition or political legitimacy, no longer justifies such hopes. Rights, deprived of life and of the fecundity of a form, are abandoned to their sheer transgressive virulence. This transgressive notion of rights has little prestige or even plausibility, however, for

Muslims who have had no positive experience of the rights of man in the framework of a nation of their own, that is, a Muslim nation.

Today, among us, in a social context where everything tends to delegitimize the national form, and even if some Muslims are not insensitive to the charms of transgression, the rights of "man separated from man" do not have much hold on moral practices that are felt to be beyond discussion. The rights of man, as these have come to be understood throughout the course of the history of European nations, will be of little help in bringing Muslims to see their moral practices reasonably from a certain distance; as we now understand them, human rights imply the pure and simple disappearance of Islam as a form of common life. Muslims are too attached to their moral practices and to their religion to give into the temptation to become "modern individuals" by disappearing as Muslims. It is nevertheless urgent that, without abandoning these practices, they put them in their place within a political form that is not limited to protecting these practices but becomes something intrinsically desirable to adhere to and to participate in. The only political form available for such a transformation of the life and of the consciousness of Muslims is the national form, the form of the old nation. In the case of the Muslims of France, this nation is France. This proposition involves many difficulties. I must try to defend it.

# 16.

Unlike most proposals for "bringing Islam into the Republic," this proposition does not set the requirement of a "reform of Islam," an emphatic and vague formula for a metamorphosis of which there are few indications and over which non-Muslims will never have more than a small influence. As I have already had the occasion to say, the "reform of Islam" is not a pertinent political question insofar as such reform has not emerged in a distinct and appreciable way in the Muslim world. The Islam that is called to participate in a political form, the nation, that today is greatly weakened, is an Islam still committed to its moral practices. How is it possible to imagine a successful meeting between a "strong" Islam and a "weak" nation?

The political and spiritual weakening of the nation in Europe is doubtless the major fact of our time. Still, there are a number of ways to consider this fact. What the stalemate of European construction has by now proved to all who are willing to believe their eyes is that Europe cannot be envisioned as a new political form that might give shelter to European life as the various nations have done up to this point. To sum up an argument that I have developed elsewhere: as weakened as it may be, the nation remains the main and decisive framework of European life. The specific problem posed by Islam only renders this framework more necessary and salutary. If Islam spreads and consolidates in a space deprived of a political form, or in which all forms of common life are delivered over to gnawing criticism from the standpoint of individual rights, now the source of all legitimacy, then there hardly remains any future for Europe but that of an Islamization by default. The term "Islamization" is apposite, for what other name can be given to the expansion and consolidation of a form of common life that would increasingly become the sole collective reference in a space otherwise devoted to the dispersion or anarchy of individual rights? One might add, moreover, that the global character of the Muslim association gives it a particular aptitude for establishing and extending itself in a space that itself has been deprived of its internal borders and that is loathe to provide external borders. "Islamization by default" is accurate, because it proceeds by a mechanical extension, simply taking advantage of the spontaneous or deliberate collapse of all the associations that used to give form and salience to the life of European nations. This is an Islamization that both Muslims and the old inhabitants of Europe are *undergoing* because the former came here for the most part to find better living conditions, and the latter never had the chance to accept or to refuse Muslim immigration, since the official interpretation of rights dictated that Muslims be considered exclusively as rights-bearing individuals and in no way as bearers of a collective form. This Islamization by default is the latent truth of our situation. No one can say what circumstance might bring about its crystallization. It is clear that we prefer not to see this latent truth, for no one knows how he will conduct himself in the new order of things in which Islam ceases to be a reality that is covered over and merely inconvenient or disconcerting and becomes an open and determining reality. Neither Muslims nor others are ready for the ordeal of truth, but we sense that we are at the mercy of some internal or external incident. It is important to take advantage of the time allowed us in order to try to make the transition from a passive coexistence between the society of rights and an Islamic morality to the active participation of both groups in a common political form that can only be the national form.

What resources are still available for such a project? Where can a nation so weakened find the political and spiritual means to rise to the height of such an unexpected and arduous task? It is notable, first, that the weakness of our nations is mainly and even exclusively a political and moral weakness. When considered as a complex of material realities and parameters – scenic landscapes, cities, infrastructures, public health, average prosperity, population statistics, etc. – France is not in bad shape. The only domain of material weakness, quite an important one to be sure, is the decline of her agricultural and industrial independence. This last is as much a moral as a material factor, since it results from a decision, or from a sequence of decisions, which we are not the only ones to have taken, which we like to call simply necessary, and which in any case derive from a certain understanding or interpretation of the bases of the world's life. The present state of the global economy has no particular relevance for the question of Islam in France, except to note that the decline of economic autarchy contributes powerfully to the downgrading of the nation as such even as it undermines concern for the nation's political and spiritual independence. We might ask ourselves, though, whether our nations will be able for much longer to flaunt their indifference to independence and their confidence in the benefits of flux. One might say that the question of Islam has become prominent for us precisely at the moment when we are experiencing growing doubts concerning the merits of economic denationalization. The high-minded indifference or the militant support that our rulers have shown towards the processes that constitute globalization, including notably migration, has run up against growing distrust or hostility in Europe. One might say that our nations' citizens, after having experienced the relaxation of concern for the common good, at once as a relief from tension and as the attainment of a higher level of morality, and having envisioned the abandonment of the burden of sovereignty even as a deliverance, now with apprehension see the time approaching when the very existence of the nation as a community of meaning and form will be put radically in question. If we look at France in particular, we are reminded that the years that followed the end of Gaullism, that is, in effect, the years after the death of President Pompidou, have seen a loss of energy and a weakening of all rules, in both public and private life. This has been a very mild renunciation, but one that cannot continue beyond a certain point. The proposition that I am advancing might therefore also make a claim to necessity or rather urgency. My point is not to propose something that seems desirable to a certain number of citizens whose imagination has taken a certain turn; it is rather to know whether the nation, precariously suspended between persevering in being and allowing itself to be broken up by force and flux, can still be the framework and the agent of a deliberation and an action that open up a desirable and meaningful future for all its citizens. The Muslims of France considered as a group or community represent the unprecedented obstacle that at once renders the process especially arduous and requires us to awaken latent resources and to give reality to buried and forgotten possibilities.

I have emphasized repeatedly – and this in a way constitutes the main critical proposition of this essay – that our political regime has progressively brought about its own paralysis by the ever narrower and more unilateral way it has understood its principles. The rights of man have been separated radically from the rights of the citizen and, instead of freeing members of society in order to make them capable and desirous of participating in what is common, they are now supposed to suffice to themselves, and public institutions are nothing more than their docile instrument. We are probably the first, and we will surely remain the only, people in history to give over all elements of social life and all contents of human life to the unlimited sovereignty of the individual. Here is not the place to examine the causes and the meaning of such a strange development. It is important, nevertheless, to emphasize to what degree such a transformation of the criteria of the just tends to deprive any perspective on life and common action of legitimacy and meaning. As I have said, what is at work under the term "equality" or "secularism," or under the formula "values of the Republic," is the disqualification of all shareable contents of life for not having been chosen by each individual, or because they do not please each individual. It is easy to see that, if humanity had begun its adventure by embracing such principles, neither families, nor cities, nor religious communities would ever have been created. Strangely, our regime has taken on the task of drawing support more and more exclusively from a principle upon which it happens to be impossible to found anything at all. The reasoning goes something like this: if we want the French, in their diversity, which it is now impossible to gather into a unity, to live together according to the equality of rights, then they must have nothing in common except the values of the Republic, that is, the dispositions that make it possible to live together without having anything in common. We will survive as a community of life and of meaning only if we awaken from this vertigo of dissolution.

The production of common things always holds a part of mystery. The diversity of common things produced by humanity is the object of wonder and admiration. The diversity of common things produced throughout European history is particularly surprising and admirable. I have sought the conditions of this incomparable fecundity in the need to articulate the indeterminacy of the political regime and form along with the indeterminacy of the response to be given to the Christian proposition of an alliance between human freedom and divine benevolence. Each form of common life in Europe was a way of resolving this double indeterminacy by in a way linking the concretization of a way of governing oneself with the concretization of a certain relation to the Christian proposition. Have we left behind this political and religious matrix? In any case, it has been a long time since we built an enormous artifice, an enormous instrument, that essentially renders imaginable and, so to speak, desirable the leaving behind of the political and religious order, and that seems to promise this double emancipation.

What, in effect, is the modern state, the sovereign and liberal state, if not this extraordinary instrument that both tends to strip the diversity of regimes and of political forms of all relevance and to insert itself between man and God, or to make itself God? It tends to deny the relevance or importance of the question of the regime or political form because, by guaranteeing members of society the enjoyment of their rights, it seems to dispense them from having to govern themselves. It inserts itself between man and God, or it makes itself a God, because, by abstracting itself from the society where human beings live, and by offering itself as the sovereign author of the human order, it assumes the high ground and arrogates to itself the task reserved to divine Providence. The "secular" state, from which we now expect miracles and whose political and spiritual weakness I have emphasized, is but the presumptuous and bloodless heir of the modern state, which was once so strong. What is important for our argument is to remember that the modern State at its greatest strength never succeeded in delivering Europeans either from the question of the regime and of political form, or from that of the relationship with Christianity, which on the contrary gave the state legitimacy and finality, and multiplied and varied the bases of its power. It was from peoples' seeking the best means to govern themselves in obedience to divine government that the modern State drew its resources and nourished its ambition to replace the government of men as well as the government of God. This functional ambivalence of the state, which is the ambivalence of an "unlimited instrument," is inseparably a moral and a spiritual ambivalence, for the state can be successively and sometimes simultaneously impartial master and furious tyrant, intelligent servant and blind slave.

We no longer have what it takes to confront such ambiguities, or even to recognize them. We dream of an instrument ready to hand that would nevertheless always have enough power and justice to be exquisitely impartial and intelligent, thus relieving us of the obligation to govern ourselves. The construction of Europe gave some plausibility and some equally provisional popularity to what was called "governance," which is really only *government by the State alone*, or by the purest and most abstract form of the State, a State delivered from the ambiguity of its condition and of its meaning. The governance that wraps itself in the European cloak amounts to the exercise of the power to command by an apparatus that is entirely detached from the political order, that is, from any regime as well as from any political form. This is a power that obviously no longer has anything in common with representative government, since such government is inseparable from a people to be represented. Governance is also, of course, entirely detached from the concern for the divine, or in general from the question of the truth concerning the human order. A power without either origin or purpose hovers between two worlds that it believes it has left behind, when in fact it is at their mercy.

# 17.

The invocation of secularism, of the values of the Republic, or of European governance – all essentially synonymous expressions – thus leaves gapingly open the two major questions that must be taken into account if one wishes finally to return to the element in which we actually live, that is, the question of the regime and the religious question.

The question of the regime is the simpler question, if not to solve then at least to characterize. It is urgent to recover a representative regime beyond the already tired illusions of European governance. A representative government presupposes a people to represent. The representable people of Europe takes the concrete form of the plurality of the peoples of the various European nations, each of these peoples having and wishing to have its representative government. The governments of Europe are responsible to their respective peoples, and not to the European Idea, for Europe has no real existence except in the collaboration or friendship of its different nations, and not in a "European unity" that has only an ideological and bureaucratic existence. Concerning France, we know how the French have lost confidence in their elected officials at the same time as these officials have felt less and less responsible to the French people, a people that they had intended to lead as rapidly as possible to its glorious disappearance in the European ecstasy. This inconvenient people is still here. It still demands to be governed by a government in which it might still feel a minimum of confidence. This confidence was lost partly because of the European distraction: the conviction that "the real solutions" could only be found or given effect "at the level of Europe" entailed the systematic deferral of the most urgent decisions, and, in general, a lack of interest on the part of the governing class in the real life of the inhabitants of this country and in the needs inscribed in its nature and its history, a lack that was both stupid and cruel.

France's Muslims are like its other citizens: they need a representative government, not of Muslims in particular but of the French people as a whole. Do they feel this need, or would they be content to be left in peace with their way of life? Or do they see themselves as on the margins and so to speak in secession? Such questions, and many others of the same kind, are particularly hard to answer, because the civic engagement of Muslims is timid, because our regime itself, as I have just emphasized, has lost many of its representative virtues, and because it thus gives citizens little incentive to relate actively and passionately to what we hold in common. If the chasm that has opened up between citizens and their government is to be overcome, this can only be at the outset by the initiative of the latter, and more generally of the political domain. It falls naturally to those who rule to make a beginning. This is particularly true in this case, since the specificity and the acuity of the problem reside first of all in what I have called the passivity and the taciturn quality of the Muslims.

The initiative that would be most likely to forge the relationship of representation and to engage an animated civic conversation, and one that would be illuminating for all concerned, would consist in *commanding* France's Muslims to establish their independence from the various Muslim countries that send out imams, and that finance and sometimes administer or guide the mosques. This is not only or even mainly a question of "principle," since the principle of national independence, we all know, is very laxly honored in our country. It is first of all a question of political sincerity addressed to all parties. The point is for each party to the debate to show that it is serious and to this end to take certain actions that cost something and that show a commitment. If I emphasize that our political authorities must *command* Muslims to do something, this is not because I am keen to subject or re-subject these Muslims to "our" commanding authority, but rather because we yearn for a government at last capable of making hard decisions, and that this presents a decision, or a series of decisions that are among the most difficult to make. This, in any case, does not at all exclude, but in fact would instead require, the most patient spirit of negotiation and of moderation. This decision, or this series of decisions, would contribute more than anything else to defining our relation to Islam, a relation which, as I have said, has this specific quality: it concerns inseparably what is within and what is outside the political body, the internal and the external. By taking this step, the political body would effectively engage the rise of Islam as an internal and an external phenomenon; it would effectively become aware of it and would be acting according to this awareness by a measure that is inseparably defensive with respect to external Islam and friendly, albeit authoritarian, towards internal Islam. Everyone knows that many mosques and Muslim associations are largely dependent on a foreign sponsor or inspiration, and beneficiaries of foreign funds, whether these various influences come from Saudi Arabia, from Morocco, from Turkey, or from another country. It seems legitimate to demand, for example, that these funds be considerably reduced if not completely eliminated, especially since many other resources for the maintenance of places of worship and the endowment of cultural and charitable associations are available to France's Muslims, whether in the form of donations from the faithful, of the product of the halal certification or of aid from local bodies. This aid is hardly in conformity with the law of 1905, but it is adequately justified by the needs of the concerned populations, on the condition, precisely, that it make these populations materially and morally independent of foreign organizations and countries. It is by conducting this crucial policy with perseverance that a government actually concerned with the common good might give effect to the deliberately *defensive* disposition of which I have spoken since the beginning of this essay, while at the same time encouraging a mutual confidence that now hardly exists between Muslims and other citizens. Despite an often-heard objection, such a defensive position does not imply that one considers Islam to be an enemy. It is, on the contrary, the most judicious way to see that enmity does not take root. If we continue to exempt this specific character of Islam, which is precisely the "imperial" lack of a distinction between the internal and the external, from obedience to the national political order, then we will have already accomplished an act of political and therefore spiritual submission that we will not be able to reconsider. If we continue to accept the continuity, in terms of finances and personnel, between a part of French Muslims and, for example and especially, Saudi Arabia and its Wahhabist organizations, then it is vain or simply insincere to demand equal access for Muslims to the right and duties of French citizenship, even as we leave them in material and spiritual dependence in relation to that part of the Muslim world that is most foreign to our notions of what is just and good.

This requirement of *obedience to commands*, these dispositions that I have called authoritarian, can only have the desired effect if they are finally met with the consent and approval of the concerned persons among French Muslims. There is no question that this will not be easy, and that there will be successes and failures. There will no doubt be many diplomatic complications. It is precisely by mastering all these elements that the government and the nation will show themselves capable at once of generously welcoming new Muslim citizens and of defending itself against the external pressure of Islam. This pressure, moreover, is more and more directly effective on the whole of the political body and in particular on its elites, whose indulgence towards an actor as suspect as Qatar is a daily object of wonder. It goes without saying that it will be hard to impose the restrictions I recommend on France's Muslims, since some of the most prestigious national institutions find the Gulf countries to be supplementary sources of funding that the general budgetary woes render so enticing.

I have noted that some deplore the local public funding of the construction of mosques or the maintenance of Muslim cultural associations as an infringement of the law of 1905. They demand that the law be applied. These complaints are ill considered. This funding will continue because it is part of the continual negotiation that localities must conduct with this part of the population they administer, as with others. If it were eliminated in order to obey the law, this measure would only lead to and essentially justify the growth of much more corrupting funding by foreign institutions and countries, to say nothing of the increased role that would be assumed by opaque commercial networks. Here we have an illustration that is as concrete as one could wish for of the general proposition maintained in these pages, that is, that "secularism" offers us only an imaginary policy, one that surely allows us to "take a position" but that in no way guides public action in a way that takes account of current conditions. We have not yet elaborated on what institutions would be adapted to these conditions, but such institutions could only be the result of an action that would take them adequately into account.

The measures that I recommend, and that are no less difficult for the government to enact than for many of the concerned citizens to accept (to say nothing of the concerned foreign countries), will be at stake in the test of strength between the two groups and within each of them. On the one hand, this test will allow us to determine whether we still have a government and whether it is capable of stipulating the elementary conditions of common life. On the other, it will oblige French Muslims to make a major choice that is public and deliberate, a step that they have never had the occasion to take, and one that would be much more significant for them and for us than this "adaptation" of their religion that we insist on demanding from them. Rather than hiding the signs of their religious affiliation, a weak and equivocal gesture, they would enter into the public square as they are, that is, as French Muslims capable of bringing about the French nation's acceptance of their Muslim commitments and the rest of the Muslim world's acceptance of their French commitments. I will not attempt to evaluate the probability or the plausibility of the unprecedented gestures that I am outlining, since such founding or re-founding acts are by definition unpredictable, breaking as they do with all settled political, social and moral ways. Contrary to what the lazy prevailing morality is sure to suggest, the rule that I call for does not at all make the active participation of Muslims in national life more difficult; it is rather the first condition for such participation. Far from showing them a lack of respect, it declares them to be desirable and welcome. The indifference that asks nothing of them under the pretext of respect in fact abandons them, and abandons us as well, to a general demoralizing passivity.

I am not foretelling the history of the next five or ten years, but neither am I living in the land of chimera. I am looking for an active way out the increasingly thorny encounter of two passive groups. Islam is passive in the immobility of its moral practices and in its reluctance to venture beyond the perimeter of the community. Europe is passive in its surrender to all the processes that pervade it or affect it. This contact without real communication, this separation that has no spiritual meaning, since both sides are afraid to think about the meaning of things – all this promises only an indifference so profound that it will have nothing to oppose to the passions of distrust and enmity if circumstances provide such passions with a cause and an occasion. Only an encounter that is active on both sides will revive the representative vigor of our regime, the government demanding representative authority over the Muslims of France, and these Muslims demanding to be accepted not only as equal rights-bearing individuals but as a community that henceforth has its place in the French public square, and whose attachment to the Muslim religion is free of all slavish dependence on the powers that dominate the rest of the Muslim world. Only a France activated in this way, or a Europe so activated in its nations, and only an Islam so activated as a collective agent, will be capable of discouraging and as it were of disqualifying the acts of war that the passivity of these two worlds favors or foments. There is good reason to say that "the immense majority of France's Muslims are peaceful," but this tranquility is also a political and intellectual passivity that prevents them from taking adequate account of their situation and from responding to it judiciously. We are in this together; the opportunities and the risks are equally shared. If we fail, that will mean both that our regime has entirely lost the representative virtue that had defined and animated it since its founding, and that France's Muslims are incapable of moving beyond the immobility of their moral practices in order to nourish a political desire, that is, in order to experience effectual freedom as Muslims. Of course each side will blame the other for its failure, and each will be right and wrong at the same time.

# 18.

As I have said, the question whether or not the Muslims will as Muslims experience effectual freedom depends on whether or not our regime recovers its virtue. This formula will no doubt be blamed for being equivocal or contradictory. It will be said that it is precisely through the experience of effectual freedom that the Muslims will detach themselves from an excessively burdensome Muslim identity in order, while still remaining Muslims, to become free citizens, since citizenship is precisely this process of detachment from affiliations. The citizen as such is neither Muslim, nor Jew, nor Christian, nor a member of some other community of opinion or of any other religion, but a member precisely only of the community of citizens. This thesis is very true, but it easily misleads us if we follow it to the letter. Indeed, if we follow it to the letter, it tends to destroy itself. Let us say that the activity of citizenship tends to detach the citizen from all prior attachments. What happens to the community of citizens to which he also belongs? Does it not also constitute an attachment? Does not citizenship understood as a "stripping of all attachments" tend to destroy citizenship? This is in any case how one might interpret the profound change of meaning that the notion has undergone in recent times. The "citizen" of today is someone who has understood that citizenship cannot be circumscribed by a national attachment, since this most often depends on birth. The true citizen henceforth is one who is detached from all community, even the civic community, and who bears his various memberships as so many ties that do not bind. The understanding of citizenship as detachment or breaking free leads irresistibly to the absorption of the rights of the citizen by the rights of man, and to the formation of a new figure, that of the citizen-individual, who defines himself by the freedom always to reconsider his attachments, including his civic attachment, and thus by the permanent freedom of the breaking of bonds. When we proclaim the attachment of all to the values of the Republic, this must in truth be understood as proposing values without a Republic, or values of a Republic without any common good, since a common good implies belonging, common education, loyalty and devotion to what is common, none of which we intend to allow to bind us.

Thus, when we are asked to adhere to the values of the Republic, *nothing* is asked of us. The result is that everyone likes to proclaim these values, a money that may buy nothing, but at least costs nothing to print. Nothing is asked of us, or at least nothing is asked but abstentions, something of which even the laziest citizen is always capable. In practice, the citizen is asked only not to speak ill of his neighbor, and if possible not to think of him at all. In psychological terms, he is asked especially to *relax*, not to take any public matter seriously, because a public matter is the occasion for, or rather motivates, engagement, tension, seriousness, judgment. A public matter is a difficult thing that occasions difficulties. In truth, the new citizenship consists in demobilizing the affects of citizenship, and it is this demobilization that has delivered the social atmosphere over to ubiquity, or to the contagious panic of *identification*: the "I" imagines that it can identify itself with all things as it pleases, and identify all things with itself. A civic world, a world in which things are held in common, is a world in which identification with something other than one's own community of belonging is not only difficult but impossible. A person cannot form several equally serious identifications with communities of the same type or rank. The complex of identifications that make up one's personality, such as the identification with one's family, one's party, one's religion, one's nation, changes very slowly if it changes at all, and this change always involves crisis and pain. To "leave the party," to abandon one's religion or convert to another, to renounce one party, to divorce – these are all trials for any human being of any substance. The "Republic of values" is an indefinitely elastic human grouping, in which we do not know with whom or with what one might ask us or we might somehow wish to "identify" ourselves tomorrow.

This is not the kind of society in which Muslims will find their place. Citizenship cannot mean detachment, much less tearing away, from the religious community, either for them or for the other members of the civic body. French Catholics are not torn away from their religion in order to become citizens, or to "rally" to the Republic. It is true that they have had some difficulty combining French citizenship with Church membership. This shows that at least they have taken the two cities seriously. They were, and for that matter are still, at once French citizens and "children of the Church." They were and they are these things *inseparably*. This is so true that in times of trial the roles are spontaneously switched, the Church being also a city for which one dies, and France being loved like a mother: "Oh, mother, such as we are, we are here to serve you."[7] Muslims will become truly citizens, not by separating or abstracting themselves from their religion, but by seeing themselves *as Muslims* as members of the national community. If the nation in a certain sense detaches them from their religion, since they share it with non-Muslims, it immediately gives it back to them, and they receive it now in a way from the nation in which they have finally found, not only a place, but their place. Only through such a spiritual movement is it possible, not to "identify oneself," but to participate in two equally demanding communities. This is the supremely delicate operation that we must carry out together.

Clearly this operation is too vast and too delicate to depend merely on the simplifying force of an institution, even if the specific representation of Muslims in France is called upon to play an important role, on the condition that this representative institution not only defends "the moral and material interests" of Muslims, but embodies their choice of France and thus their independence from the "dominating powers" of the Muslim world. This choice

---

7    Charles de Gaulle often employed this expression of Charles Péguy during World War II and in his *Mémoires de Guerre*.

of France is only possible if it is sincere. It can only be sincere if, to repeat, by giving themselves to France, Muslims receive from her in return their religion. In this exchange, which changes nothing and changes everything, the religious group experiences a shrinking and an expansion, or, in Christian terms, a humiliation and an elevation. Shrinking or humiliation, because one must accept being part of a whole; expansion or elevation because, through participation in this whole, the group accedes to something larger than itself. This operation is at once political and religious. In it, the political and the religious are articulated without being separated. The political and spiritual arrangement I am trying to define is in no way contrary, nonetheless, to the liberal or secular "separation" – in the original and precise meaning of the term "secular" ["laïque"], which in fact presupposes it. Priests do not command in the city, political leaders do not conduct prayer, and the common soul of the city is enlarged by being divided and shared in this way.

I believe these remarks make it possible to pose the question of communitarianism with somewhat more finesse. Today we tend to oppose a happy France, unified by a secular separation, from the unhappy France fragmented by communitarianism. I believe in effect that communitarianism constitutes a degraded form of religious and political life, but how exactly is it to be understood? It is true enough that communitarianism confuses religion and politics, but this is not simply or mainly because it has not accomplished or accepted the separation, but more profoundly because it has not brought to term the distinct movement that I have tried to characterize, by which the religious group gives itself as such to the political community and receives itself from that community. The communitarian group remains separated from the rest of the political body because it fears losing itself and fully participating in it; it fears that, if it gives itself, it will no longer find itself in what is common. Communitarianism is best defined by a distrust that is at once religious and political, a spiritual mistrust that affects at once the group and the whole. Communitarianism maintains souls without generosity.

I have neither the authority nor the competence to evaluate the spiritual condition of the constituent groups of our country. At the same time, it is impossible to enter into these urgent questions, at once civic and intimate, that face us with any seriousness without presupposing or implying such judgments, for it is this spiritual condition that will determine the political and religious future of the groups and of the whole that they form or do not form together. While aware of the both approximative and apparently condescending character of the proposition, I therefore risk saying that France's Muslims, although they may sometimes or often display communitarian tendencies, nevertheless have not settled into communitarianism. The question remains undecided. It has not yet been decided, because, having not yet received a credible proposal, the Muslims have had nothing to respond to. They have remained in this passivity or this reserve that I have emphasized several times. They have been left with the abstract and possibly specious choice between communitarianism and secularism understood as the neutralization of religion in society. There is no response to a specious choice. What does secularism mean for them? Must they remove the signs of their moral practices or renounce them? It seems sometimes that secularism asks almost nothing of them, and other times that it asks of them almost everything. In any case, since there is no way they can separate themselves from their moral practices, they go their own way and make no commitments.

Consider again the terms of the delicate operation I have suggested. If Muslims must offer themselves frankly and as Muslims to the political body that we form, they must reciprocally receive themselves from this body. They must receive their place as Muslims – not the place of citizens in general, but their own place. This place cannot flow merely from abstract principles, from democratic and republican "generality." It is determined through the experience of the concerned parties, thus according to the past, but also according to their perspective on the future, according to the decisions they make and will make. As for what is determined by experience up to this point, it is up to Muslims to find a place in a Christian country, or a country of a Christian mark. The situation would be completely different if they had gone from a Muslim country to another Muslim country. We cannot be satisfied to say lazily: they entered a secular country! Secularism is a governmental arrangement that does not exhaust the meaning of common life, and that, moreover, provides only an abstract and quite impoverished picture of it. One does not live a separation.

The Muslims that live in France did not go, as they might have, to a Muslim country. They came freely into a country that, if other countries are designated as Muslim, must be called Christian rather than anything else. That makes a difference. Of course they did not come in order to become Christian, even though some, a small number, do so. Why did they come? The common answer is: to live better. This is a perfectly natural and therefore a legitimate response, but one that does not define a place in the political body. If they go no further than this, they are condemned to quite an impoverished sociability: living within the immanence of their moral practices, they will look at France rather as a foreign body, more or less pleasant, more or less convenient, sometimes inconvenient. On both sides a spiritually empty heterogeneity will prevail, thus one without movement or progress. If they are to enter into national life as Muslims, they must succeed in the operation that I have tried to describe, by which the group gives itself and receives itself from the whole. In order for this to succeed, the group must take real political and religious conditions into account. It would take just a little sincerity and good sense for us not to pretend to see Muslims merely as human beings in general, but also and especially as Muslims, just as we would not pretend to see France merely as a "secular country," unless we propose making the churches and cathedrals disappear in the wrappings of the artist Christo. It is therefore in a country of a Christian mark that French Muslims must find their place. This does not make the operation more difficult, but on the contrary easier, since Muslims always consider European and more generally Western countries in these terms. Some of them, as we know, designate Europeans and Americans as "crusaders." There is more truth in this exaggeration than in our denials. To designate with precision what for them or for many of them represents the distinctiveness of our country is to introduce a bit of candor and of truth in our relationship.

For Muslims, to find a place in a Christian country, or a country marked by Christianity, does not mean accepting a subordinate place. Christians, or particularly Catholics, do not rule in France. Political rule has been rigorously separated from religious commandments and precepts enjoined by the Church; this is secularity in its proper sense, which is indeed necessary and salutary. Thus Catholics too, as I said at the outset, must accomplish the delicate operation that allows for the union without confusion between politics and religion, after or along with their separation. They too must give themselves as citizens to a civic body larger than the association of French Catholics, not to lose themselves there, but in order to take their place as Catholics. For them, too, this is a matter of accomplishing the movement of the soul that is at once a shrinking and an enlargement, humiliation and elevation. Either they will accomplish it generously, or, refusing to be just a part, and wishing secretly to rule, they will deprive themselves of the elevation and enlargement that are inseparable from a generous contribution to the common good. There is no institutional refuge, there is no partisan instrument, and there is no theological subtlety that will dispense the Catholic citizen from the process, at once civic and Christian, by which he recognizes himself as a part, gives himself to the whole, and by doing so gives this whole a spiritual character in which he can recognize himself and "glorify himself" at once as a citizen and as a Christian.

French Catholics and French Muslims, though the product of very different histories, have the same operation to accomplish. Catholics have the advantage, if it can be called that, of long experience, often painful, sometimes humiliating, sometimes glorious or at least encouraging. In calm periods, Catholics tend to neglect the delicate operation I am discussing, one that presents itself as a *trial* in moments of crisis. If they signal each other in such calm times, it is by their devotion to social needs. Such devotion is admirable in itself, but it is no substitute either for civic action or for the spiritual action by which the Christian collaborates in the communication of divine life and thus in the work of salvation. The Muslim question obligates Catholics to recover self-awareness, and to recover forgotten questions, that of their place in the political body, that of the meaning of their participation in common affairs and that of their attention to "ultimate ends" and of their confidence in Providence. Their spontaneous reaction is the chant of "forget-me-not." Do not forget us, we too are "believers" in France, and have been such for much longer than these late comers who monopolize the attention and the consideration of the political class. . . This is not enough. A long period of calm is coming to an end. A period of trial is beginning, one that will be as decisive for the subsequent physiognomy of Catholicism, and thus of France, as were the Revolution and the Second World War. Catholics can feel it. They are preparing themselves for it, as one can judge by innumerable publications or meetings dealing, on the one hand, with secularism, and on the other with Islam, the two "fronts" between which they feel threatened with suffocation, as Muslims attain a more and more significant place in the public square, while a more and more aggressive interpretation of secularism goes after the most modest traces of the presence of Christianity, this manger scene in a little station in the south, or this statue of John Paul II in a little town of Brittany. There is no doubt that Catholics make up one of the major sectors of opinion now most anxiously questioning the new situation. I have no idea what will come of the trouble and the mistrust among Catholics. I wish however to indicate what, as it seems to me, is to be feared, and what hoped for.

The first is the easier to discern. Catholics are tempted to respond to the challenges that assail them by adopting the defensive and reactive posture that was, of course, their preferred mode during the modern period. Clerics and the laity close ranks and seek refuge in the Catholic fortress, which is shrunken and damaged, to be sure, but which still has what it takes to carry on in European societies, torn as they now are between the archaic moral practices of the Muslims and the nihilism of Western ways. They can still for a long time provide the bag that everyone punches to calm one's nerves, and at the same time the ballast that prevents the French ship from listing too much. Nevertheless, this minimal response is insufficient in the face of the hazards to which a political body so fragile as ours is exposed. Like any simply reactive response, it is neither noble nor politically judicious, and, of course, in properly religious terms, it exhibits deficiencies in hope and in charity. Thus, if Catholics at least want to retain a certain composure and to be attentive to the underlying order of the theologico-political arrangement that accommodates our disorders, they will realize that their defeatism is not justified.

By theological-political arrangement I refer to the dynamic relationship sustained by the great spiritual masses of the West. The internal constitution of these masses and their sources are of prodigious complexity, but the reciprocal relation *among* these masses presents some fairly simple features, or, at least, considered in the perspective relevant to our subject, this reciprocal relation presents features that are encouragingly simple. Here is what I would say of this. The five great spiritual masses that determine the figure of the West are Judaism, Islam, Evangelical Protestantism (mainly American), the Catholic Church, and, finally, the ideology of human rights. Now, it seems to me that what characterizes and distinguishes the Catholic Church within this configuration is, if I may say, its calmness and equilibrium. The other spiritual forces, to varying degrees and for reasons that are in each case specific, are engaged in a movement of self-affirmation that is largely indifferent to the views and to the wishes of the rest of humanity. They wish to know only their own rights and their own reasons. The Catholic Church is the only spiritual force that approaches matters in such a way as to take into account the views of others in a deliberate and as it were thematic way. This is eminently the case in its relation to Judaism, as I have already suggested. The Catholic Church has not only searched its conscience in a very profound way concerning its responsibility for anti-Judaism and anti-Semitism; it has also reconsidered in depth its relation to the Jewish people. It understands that its claim to being the true and exclusive Israel not only harmed the Jewish people but also obscured the meaning and the dynamic of the covenant. Without at all abandoning the confession of faith which distinguishes and defines it, the Church admits that her eminent and singular role in the communication of truth does not imply that Israel is left only with blindness and hardness of heart. In a certain sense, the relation of the Church to the ideology of human rights is symmetrical with its relation to Judaism. For the democratic doctrine that prevails today, Christianity is only the Old Testament of true universalism, that is, the universalism contained in the Declaration of the Rights of Man, a declaration that is continuously being extended and perfected. There has been a debate within the Church for more than two centuries over this doctrine, and the Church's position has known variations of great amplitude. After having condemned it as a revolt against God, the Church more recently has tended to see it as an expression of a movement of human liberation that, in its essentially legitimate content, has its source in the Gospel. This is not the place to examine the history of these variations. What it is important for us to observe is that the Church has entered into a constant dialectical and moral debate with this doctrine, which represents at once a derivation from the Christian doctrine of the conscience and a rupture with it. We are obliged to note that this dialectical opening of the Church has not been repaid, the ideology of human rights having taken on a virulence in recent times that seems to be directed most particularly against the way of life that the Church recommends, protects, and promotes. As to the relation between the Church and Islam, I can say the following: Even if we must leave aside the irenic and ignorant statements of certain Catholics on Islam as an "Abrahamic religion," statements that are becoming rarer as a minimal knowledge of Islam spreads, it remains that it is Catholics who most often have taken the initiative of these "dialogues" in which one seeks, not only to facilitate coexistence between Catholics and Muslims, but also to give a positive meaning to religious plurality. The popes themselves, John Paul II most especially, have gone as far as possible in developing the possibility of a perspective common to Christians and to Muslims. There is, moreover, in Catholic thought a tradition of mystical proximity with Islam, or of proximity with mystical Islam, a tradition summed up in the name Massignon.[8]

In a word, while others promote themselves and their claims, the Catholic Church maintains itself, and raises questions while questioning itself. It establishes a relationship with each of the other great spiritual forces. These relationships may be more or less rich dialectically, more or less intimate or intense, but the relationship is such that it leaves each party free to be what it is, thus bearing the promise of a life in which concern for peace and the pursuit of the truth would not be incompatible. The Catholic Church will not rid itself of the imputation of intolerance that attaches to it, whatever it may say or do. Though past history provides ample justification for this accusation, it must be admitted that today the Catholic Church is the least intolerant and the most open of the spiritual forces that concern us. In particular, being alone capable of nourishing a meaningful and substantial relationship with all the other spiritual forces, it is the center or the pivot of a configuration in which we have to live and to think. It is thus the mediator *par excellence*, not in the theological sense that makes the Church, as Bossuet said, "Christ shared and communicated," but in a sense that is less defined spiritually, but very meaningful politically. The Pope has put down his tiara, and the Church no longer claims to gather humanity under its rule. Still, given the spiritual fragmentation that affects the Western world, it is the fixed point that is concerned to relate itself intelligently to all the other points, and to which the other points can try to relate.

If there is something to this analysis, certain important consequences follow for the action and the conduct of Catholics in the various European nations of which they are citizens. Again,

---

8   Louis Massignon (1883–1962) was a famous French Catholic convert and scholar of Islam who expressed great sympathy for Islamic religious traditions and who 'mystically' identified with them. It was he, above all, who emphasized the shared "Abrahamic" character of Judaism, Christianity, and Islam.

although it possesses neither the power nor the desire to rule, the Church is at the center of this configuration. Certain dispositions are appropriate to this position, the first being a sense of responsibility for the whole. Given recent developments that put "pressure" on the Church, especially in France, there is the risk of setting about being like everyone else, that is, seeing only one's own rights and reasons. It is necessary and just to defend oneself when attacked. I will not rehearse the evidence that the Church endures more than its share of attacks, but the task of Catholics lies elsewhere, and it by no means concerns only Catholics. This task follows from the responsibility for the whole that I have just emphasized, that is, a responsibility for the common good of the various spiritual forces. In practice, this means that Catholics have a special responsibility for the common good of the association in which these forces meet, that is, in our case, for the common good of France.

Among all these spiritual forces, the Catholic Church is obviously the one whose companionship with the French nation is the most extensive and deepest, or the most penetrating. This is not the place to recount the history of this companionship, or to sort out the threads of this reciprocal belonging; for, if the Church has played an axial role in the history of France, France has often played a determining role in the history of the Church. Our common history is made up not only of what the Church has done – both good and bad – to France, but also of what France has done – both good and bad – to the Church. Now that the slow weakening of the Church coincides with the abrupt weakening of the nation, their relation cannot remain one of a chest full of memories; nor can it remain a game of superficial references, one side boasting proudly of "France, the eldest daughter of the Church," and the other unable to rid its mind of the memory of Saint Bartholomew.[9]

9    On St. Bartholomew's Day, August 24, 1572, in the midst of war between Catholics and Protestants ("Huguenots") in France, Catholic forces, under the direction of Catherine de Medici, slaughtered thousands of Protestants in attacks that spread from Paris to a number of other cities.

Most important, this relationship can no longer be assigned to the category of secularism, understood according to the current interpretation, the specious character of which I have emphasized. To repeat: the secularity of the State in no way implies the secularism of society, an empty notion the mystifying function of which is shown, on the one hand, by the explicit and even institutional role of France's Jews, and, on the other, by the increasingly flagrant presence of Muslim moral practices, in the public square. Our common life will suffer from a kind of spiritual atrophy, and first of all from a profound defect of sincerity, as long as we remain incapable of publicly addressing the intimate relationship that links France to the Church. This urgent change in the tenor of the civic conversation requires no institutional change, nor even any particular steps on the part of political institutions. Everything in effect depends on the Church and on France's Christians, on their capacity to enter judiciously into civic life. Catholics have long assumed the habit of standing back, away from the action. Although secularism leaves them entirely free in their movements, they often conduct themselves as if they were condemned to a clandestine existence. But how can one leave this quasi-clandestine state without joining the prideful competition of claims and counter-claims that is the scourge of our whining age?

# 19.

One cannot respond to this question with a program or with a list of requirements. For human groups as for individuals, either they are capable of finding their good within the common good, or they fail at the common good, thus losing their own good and losing themselves. I have tried to explain why, although Catholics seem to be pushed ever further towards the periphery of public life, the Church as a spiritual domain is at the center of the Western configuration. Her responsibility is proportional to this centrality, which in truth is inseparable from her identity. Just as the universal Church seems alone up to the task of holding together the configuration that joins her with Judaism, Islam, evangelical Protestantism, and the doctrine of human rights, the Church in France, that is, French Catholics, have a special responsibility for the common good in which the other spiritual forces of our country participate. One suspects that these other forces are not necessarily informed of this special responsibility, nor disposed to recognize it. This is only fair. Those who feel responsible for the whole can only bring others to accept their special role if their own contribution to the common good is sufficiently convincing.

Let me sum up briefly the proposition that the main arguments of this essay serve to ground: France's Muslims will only find their place in French society if they find it in the nation. They will only find it in the nation if the nation accepts them according to its truth and according to their truth – not simply, therefore, as rights-bearing citizens accepting other bearers of the same rights, but as an association marked by Christianity granting a place to a form of life with which it has never before mixed on an equal footing. It is precisely because the encounter between these two forms of life has generally been so difficult and even painful, and thus because the chances for a fellow citizenship that is at last happy appear modest to those who choose not to dream, that it is important for us to be very attentive to the actual situation of those on both sides, and very sincere on both sides in the formation and the formulation of our wishes. As I have said, while our Muslim fellow citizens must obviously enjoy the rights of French citizens without any kind of discrimination, which is not always the case at present, their place as a group will still be determined qualitatively by the spiritual and political arrangement I have tried to outline. They will not enter into an empty space, but will have to find their place within a world that is full. Those who accept them have in principle the spiritual and intellectual resources to be generous without being complacent. Those who are accepted must want to participate actively in the life of a political body that does not and will not belong to the *umma*; they must therefore accept a degree of separation from the *umma*. For the nation to accept them as Muslims without reducing their religious mark to a private particularity without relevance to the political body, it is necessary that they accept this nation as the site of their civic activity, and more generally of their education. This will not happen without difficulty, on the one side as on the other. A certain "communitarianism" is inevitable. It is even desirable to the degree that it prevents the ideological lie of the new secularism, which would obligate us to pretend to be nothing but citizen-individuals.

Muslims will inevitably form a visible and tangible community within the French nation, a *distinct* community in a nation in which they are citizens *like others*. This situation will only be livable and lasting if Muslims form such a community within a surrounding community *that is not Muslim*, and that everyone knows is not Muslim. This is perhaps the time to dot the "i"s. The Republic in which all citizens have equal rights is also a nation of a Christian mark in which Jews play an eminent role. It is in this Republic that Muslims may enjoy their rights, and it in this nation that they must find their place. The more the nation is able to conserve its form, the more the Republic will be able to guarantee the equality of rights. In truth, what is asked on the one hand and on the other is a masterpiece of imagination and of moderation. We would not be volunteering for such an undertaking if we had a choice. We do not have a choice. It is too late to return from a situation that has resulted much more from our lack of reflection than from our deliberate decisions. In any case, while our failure would signify the dislocation of the nation and the inglorious end of an enduring hope, success would resonate well beyond the narrow limits of our country, since the main spiritual forces of the Atlantic and Mediterranean worlds would be concerned. This should motivate our desire for glory, if we have any left.

# 20.

Islam has sprung up in a Europe that has dismantled its ancient parapets, or has let them crumble. While speaking of nothing but roots, but no longer daring to be at home in their own countries, Europeans seek repose in movement, a movement that nothing can control or slow down. No border must be allowed to obstruct the free movement of capital, of goods, of services, of people, just as no law must circumscribe the unlimited right of individual particularity. A life without law in a world without borders – this has been the horizon of Europeans for at least a generation. Such an arrangement would seem necessarily to be quite inhospitable to Islam, which advances in the name of an absolute and divine law. As a matter of fact, Sharia law elicits much apprehension. At the same time, owing precisely to its being government by a religious law, Islam also in its own way disregards borders. The borders of both groups are thus equally indefinite. Just as Islam has never found its own political form, Europe intends to abandon the political form that is proper to it. In this meeting of two wholes deprived of political form we find the solution to the curse, or the infirmity, of being born somewhere.

How is it that Europeans have come to hate autochthony to this extent? The virulent and toxic nationalisms of the twentieth century have certainly contributed to this very general and very powerful affect. Still, the nation understood as exclusive valorization of one's own people and homicidal aversion for people from elsewhere has little to do with the political form within which Europe arose and deployed its material and spiritual powers. How do we manage to confuse the community of "blood and soil" with the political nation and with spiritual communion? We think, feel, and often act as if we were confronted with the alternative between autochthony and rootlessness, and of course we choose rootlessness, under the name of globalization or free exchange, out of horror of a *volkisch* autochthony. Our imagination as well as our memory is failing us. As long as the European nation was feeling its strength, as long as it preserved its spiritual integrity, Europeans knew nothing of this alternative. They did not have to choose between autochthony and rootlessness. I have already emphasized the original indeterminacy of this unprecedented political form, as well as the enormous element of adventure that characterized its development. This prodigiously free and diverse adventure was supported by two equally powerful principles of order and energy, the reciprocal collaboration and moderation of which gave European creativity the long arc and the richness of nuance that are unequaled in history. These two principles are, again, on the one hand, confidence in its own strength, pagan ardor and pride, if you will, and, on the other hand, confidence in the inexhaustible and imponderable benevolence of God, a benevolence offered to each and every person, a confidence proper to the Christian faith. Europe was great through its nations when it was able to mix Roman virtues, courage, and prudence, with a faith in a God who is friend to every person. Each person wished at once to "acquire the world," as Machiavelli put it, and to remain worthy of the benevolence of an impartial God. Of course this involved a great deal of misery, cruelty, and disaster, of which our depleted souls never tire of drawing the inventory. But to make the effort to measure up to the immense historical arc thus traced by the nations of Europe is to open one's soul to a breadth, height, and depth of the human enterprise that suggest by contrast how this arc was broken. The collapse into violent immanence that characterized the twentieth century derived from the weakening of Christian mediation, when nations, especially the youngest and most powerful, and those for which the mark of Christianity was, moreover, profoundly troubled by the duality of confessions, claimed to be immediate expressions of humanity itself, and each its highest and soon exclusive expression. Refusing to locate their freedom in a spiritual order ultimately connected with the power and goodness of God, they sought, ever further from the common heaven, the secret of a singular election, which they disdained henceforth to receive and to share.

We will not repair the break in the European arc. We will not take up again the long sentence at the point at which it was interrupted almost exactly a century ago. Nor is there any future either in "the construction of Europe," so badly named, for there is no architecture and nothing European on this immense empty plain where so many are said to be equal and alike fail to produce anything in common. And yet we are not without resources, both old and new. In a certain sense, we experience an embarrassment of riches that we do not know how to set in order. These are the various spiritual forces that I have tried in this essay to relate to one another, without, I hope, losing sight of the great indeterminacy of our moral and political landscape. Only a legislator or a prophet, or a prophet legislator, would dare propose a definite re-ordering of these forces. For my part, I will risk one last remark by way of conclusion.

There is no future for Europeans, either on the side of autochthony, even if one is necessarily born in some place, nor on the side of rootlessness, even if, as Montesquieu said, communication among peoples produces "great goods." We have confined ourselves to this deadly alternative because we have established ourselves within immanence as the true place of humanity. If we are but terrestrial vegetables, in effect we are left with only the choice between being rooted and being uprooted. And yet the history of Europe, as I have emphasized, is unintelligible if one does not take into account a very different notion, a notion elaborated by ancient Israel, reconfigured by Christianity and lost when the European arc was broken. This notion, without which the history of Europe is unintelligible, has itself become unintelligible to contemporary Europeans. In their eyes, this is simply contrary or foreign to reason. Whoever mentions such things by this very act leaves beyond the domain of rational communication and, one can say, democracy itself. I am speaking, of course, of the Covenant. This is not a simply rational notion, to be sure, but it is not exactly a religious dogma. It is a certain way of understanding human action in the word and in the Whole, of understanding at once its greatness and its precariousness. "God" is here the one who gives victory, but who also chastises lack of measure, who confers widely this excess of good on actions that makes them truly good, and prevents the bad from taking the evil they bear to the limit. In brief, as great as man is in his pride as a free agent, his action is inscribed in an order of the good that he does not produce and an order of grace upon which he ultimately depends. It is in the relation sealed between God and his people in ancient Israel that the notion of the Covenant found its type. Let us simply say, for present purposes, that the Covenant opens up a history of freedom, that it authorizes and so to speak motivates the greatest human enterprises, while inscribing these deeds in a relation in which humanity gathers itself in order to be tried, to know itself and to submit itself to judgment.

I have emphasized how much an important part of contemporary Judaism looks at this notion with distrust. *Where is God?* said Elie Wiesel's companion at Auschwitz. This is a natural and so to speak irresistible movement of the soul. Still, if we remain under the absolute power of this experience, what will become essentially criminal is human action as such. Humanity, especially in Europe, finds itself under Condemnation. Islam, for its part, does not know how to enter into a moral world that makes no sense to it for two reasons: on the one hand, its relation to God, consisting wholly in obedience, ignores the Covenant; on the other, having nothing to do with the destruction of European Jews, Muslims are hardly able to be sensitive to the infinitely poignant drama playing out between Europe and the Jewish people. The question whether or not the Covenant has been abrogated can have no meaning for them, and it is not by forcing them to participate in a process they have nothing to do with that we will bring about the coming together of the spiritual communities that make up European life. It is up to Christians to renew the meaning and the credibility of the Covenant. They will not do this by addressing theological arguments to Israel nor by inviting Islam to join a vague fraternity of the children of Abraham. They will renew the meaning and credibility of the Covenant only by renewing the meaning and credibility of the human association that bore the Covenant until the European arc was broken, that is, the nation. Now that the Jewish people have taken the form of a nation in Israel, the nations of Christian Europe cannot break with the national form without fatally wounding the legitimacy of Israel. While the walls of the Arab-Muslim world crumble and Muslims seem to have more and more difficulty producing a political form from their own resources, to admit them into, or rather to abandon them in a Europe without either form or common good would be to take away their best chance for a civic life. To declare or even to guarantee the rights of human beings is not sufficient to bring men together. They need a form of common life. The future of the nation of a Christian mark is a cause that brings us all together.

# Index

Also available from
St. Augustine's Press

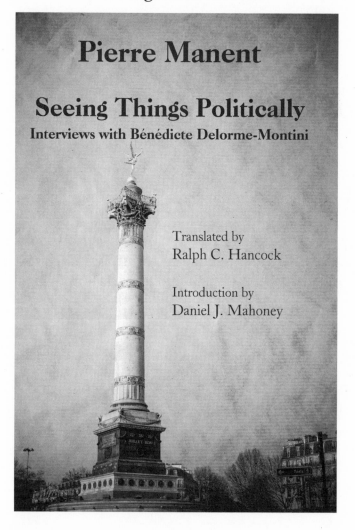

Pierre Manent

Seeing Things Politically
Interviews with Bénédicte Delorme-Montini

Translated by
Ralph C. Hancock

Introduction by
Daniel J. Mahoney